13-61

THE BERKELEY SERIES IN AMERICAN HISTORY

The Debate
Over
The Constitution
1787-1789

Edited by

ALFRED YOUNG
NORTHERN ILLINOIS UNIVERSITY

RAND McNALLY & COMPANY · CHICAGO

The Berkeley Series in American History
Charles Sellers, editor

JK
268
.Y6

CONTENTS

PAGE

INTRODUCTION   1

I. THE LINE-UP: FOR WHOM DID THE DEBATERS SPEAK?   3
   A. New York   3
     1. The Federalist Version
     Alexander Hamilton. "Conjectures about the New
     Constitution," September, 1787   4
     2. The Anti-Federalist Version   5
       a. Melancton Smith. *An Address to the People* (1788)   5
       b. James Hughes. Letter to John Lamb, June 18, 1788   5
     3. A Description of a New York City Parade. *New York Packet*, August 5, 1788   6
   B. Virginia   8
     1. The Federalist Version   9
       a. James Madison. Letters to Thomas Jefferson, December 8, 1787, April 22, 1788   9
       b. George Washington. Letter to the Marquis de Lafayette, June 19, 1788   10
     2. The Anti-Federalist Version. Patrick Henry. Letter to John Lamb, June 9, 1788   10

II. VIRGINIA: PATRICK HENRY VS. JAMES MADISON. THE QUESTION OF "STATES' RIGHTS"   12
   A. A "Consolidated" or a "Mixed" Government? Elliot, ed., *The Debates in the Several State Conventions, on the Adoption of the Constitution*   13
   B. The Power of the Purse. Elliot, ed., *Debates*   17
   C. The Question of Slavery. Elliot, ed., *Debates*   20

III. NEW YORK: ALEXANDER HAMILTON VS. MELANCTON SMITH. THE QUESTION OF "DEMOCRACY"   22
   A. How Many Representatives in the House? Elliot, ed., *Debates*   23
   B. Rule by the "Middling Classes" or the "Aristocracy"? Elliot, ed., *Debates*   27

CONTENTS

IV. THE ANTI-FEDERALISTS DIVIDE. THE QUESTION OF AMENDMENTS   34
- *A.* Melancton Smith Votes for Ratification   34
  - 1. Melancton Smith's Goals. Letter to Nathan Dane, June 28, 1788   34
  - 2. Melancton Smith's Explanation. Speech to the Convention, July 23, 1788   34
- *B.* The Amendments Anti-Federalists Wanted. Proposals of the New York Convention, July 26, 1788   36
- *C.* Abraham Yates Objects to the Results   43
  - 1. An Open Letter to the Members of the Legislature, December 8, 1788.   43
  - 2. "History of the Movement for the Constitution," Spring, 1789.   43
  - 3. An article by "Rough Hewer," March 15, 22, 1790.   44

V. NEITHER FEDERALIST NOR ANTI-FEDERALIST   47
- *A.* Thomas Jefferson Asks for a Bill of Rights   47
  - 1. Jefferson to Madison: "What I Like"; "What I do not like." Letter to Madison, December 20, 1787.   48
  - 2. Madison to Jefferson: "The Inefficacy of Parchment Barriers." Letter to Jefferson, October 17, 1788   51
  - 3. Jefferson to Madison: "A Brace to Keep up the Building." Letter to Madison, March 15, 1789   51
- *B.* Thomas Paine Asks for "A Hoop for the Barrel." "A Letter to George Washington," July 30, 1796   53

FOR FURTHER READING   55

INTRODUCTION

MANY AMERICANS WHO TODAY TAKE FOR GRANTED THAT THE FEDERAL Constitution is a "good thing" are surprised to learn that it was the subject of bitter conflict when it was first submitted to the people in 1787–1788. Some of the best known patriots of the Revolution were against its ratification, among them Patrick Henry of Virginia, Governor George Clinton of New York, and Samuel Adams of Massachusetts, while other famous leaders, such as Thomas Jefferson and Thomas Paine, had serious reservations about it.

The Founding Fathers completed the drafting of the Constitution at the Philadelphia Convention in September, 1787. For the next ten months the controversy raged as Federalists, the proponents of the Constitution, fought the anti-Federalists to win ratification in the state conventions. Consent of nine out of thirteen states was necessary for ratification. By June, 1788, eight states had agreed, but the remaining ratifications did not come easily. The two key "hold-out" states ratified it after bitter fights and by close convention votes: Virginia, eighty-nine to seventy-nine, and New York, thirty to twenty-seven. Rhode Island and North Carolina did not ratify until after the new government was set up.

The aim of this collection of original writings is to present a sampling of opinion in the great debate of 1787–1788 by focusing on Virginia and New York and on a half-dozen major political leaders of the day.

To understand the debate it makes sense to know something about the debaters. The writings in Chapter I have been selected to help answer the questions: Who were the Federalists and anti-Federalists? For whom did the debaters in Virginia and New York speak?

Chapter II focuses on one of the major issues in the Virginia convention, what today would be called the question of "states' rights." Was the new government too "centralized" and too "consolidated" or were the interests of the individual states protected? The debaters are James Madison, the "father of the constitution," and Patrick Henry, the most effective anti-Federalist orator of his day.

Chapter III takes up the question of "democracy" that ran through the New York debate, in particular whether the proposed system of representation in Congress would adequately express the opinions of the common man. The debaters are Alexander Hamilton, who had just helped write *The Federalist* essays, and Melancton Smith, "the Patrick Henry of New York" and the most cogent anti-Federalist of his state.

In and out of the conventions the decision facing men was more complicated than outright acceptance or outright rejection of the Constitution as it was submitted. Chapter IV deals with the division among anti-Federalists and Melancton Smith's reluctant decision in the final showdown to vote for, and not against, ratification. Chapter V deals with the decisions of two patriots then in France, Thomas Jefferson and Thomas Paine, who had serious objections to the Constitution yet gave it their support.

As the present-day reader works his way through these opinions he should prepare to answer the question: If I had had to make a decision on the Constitution in 1788, what stand would I have taken? The choice is not a simple one. Presented herein are the opinions of two Federalists, Madison and Hamilton, each different; two anti-Federalists, one of whom, Patrick Henry, was a bitter holdout against the Constitution, and one of whom, Melancton Smith, reversed himself; and two men, Jefferson and Paine, who were neither Federalist nor anti-Federalist.

Before beginning the debate, the reader would do well to familiarize himself with the old Articles of Confederation government and the Constitution of 1787 and should be prepared to turn to the relevant clauses in the Constitution as the debaters refer to them.

THE LINE-UP: FOR WHOM DID
THE DEBATERS SPEAK?

IN RECENT YEARS, HISTORIANS HAVE BEEN EMBROILED IN THEIR OWN CON-
troversy about how the social classes, economic interest groups, and
geographic sections were aligned in the ratification controversy. In light
of this disagreement there perhaps is something to be said for turning
to what the political participants themselves wrote about the two sides.
There is a danger, to be sure, that men who are trying to win people
to their side will exaggerate for political purposes or that they will see
only what they want to see. On the other hand, in their private corres-
pondence with their co-workers, skilled politicians usually cannot afford
to delude themselves as to who is for them and who is against them.
Even appeals made in public help to identify the groups they were
speaking to or speaking for.

The excerpts in this section are from private reports or public appeals written by men who took part in the battles in New York and
Virginia. For each of the documents the reader might ask these
questions:

1. How does the writer report the line-up of groups, classes, and
individuals?

2. For whom does he claim to speak or with whom does he identify
himself?

3. Is the writer's analysis confirmed by or contradicted by his
opponent's analysis?

4. Assuming that it is possible to conclude that one side represented
a particular group—"the yeomanry," "the mechanics," "the merchants,"
or "the aristocracy"—does this make that side's arguments any more
or less valid?

A.

NEW YORK

❡In New York the conflict over the Constitution was intense. The
state was dominated in the 1780's by the anti-Federalists. Since 1777

their leader, George Clinton, had been repeatedly re-elected Governor with the support of the state's small independent farmers and over the opposition of most of the well-to-do merchants and great estate holders of the Hudson Valley. The state sent to the Philadelphia Convention two anti-Federalists, who left in anger after a few weeks, and one Federalist, Alexander Hamilton. In the spring of 1788, the state elected forty-six anti-Federalists and nineteen Federalists to its own ratifying convention. The total vote, as well as it can be calculated, was about 16,000 anti-Federalist to 7,000 Federalist. The Federalist delegates were from New York City, a large commercial center, and the surrounding southern counties, Queens, Kings, Richmond, and Westchester, while the anti-Federalists represented Suffolk on Long Island and the counties stretching north along the Hudson and west along the Mohawk valleys.

1. *The Federalist version. Alexander Hamilton's analysis.* In this unpublished memorandum Hamilton set down a clearcut analysis of the two sides which might very well apply to his own state. ("Conjectures about the New Constitution," probably September 17–30, 1787, in Harold Syrett, ed., *The Papers of Alexander Hamilton* [New York: Columbia Univ. Press, 1962. Reprinted with the permission of the publisher.], IV, 275–76.) The numbering has been added.]

THE NEW constitution has in favour of its success these circumstances [1] a very great weight of influence of the persons who framed it, particularly in the universal popularity of General Washington [2] the good will of the commercial interest throughout the states which will give all its efforts to the establishment of a government capable of regulating protecting and extending the commerce of the Union [3] the good will of most men of property in the several states who wish a government of the union able to protect them against domestic violence and the depredations which the democratic spirit is apt to make on property; and who are besides anxious for the respectability of the nation [4] the hopes of the Creditors of the United States that a general government possessing the means of doing it will pay the debt of the Union [5] a strong belief in the people at large of the insufficiency of the present confederation to preserve the existence of the Union and of the necessity of the union to their safety and prosperity [6] of course a strong desire of a change and a predisposition to receive well the propositions of the Convention.

Against its success is to be put [1] the dissent of two or three important men in the Convention; who will think their characters pledged to defeat the plan [2] the influence of many *inconsiderable* men in possession of considerable offices under the state governments who will fear a diminution of their consequence, power and emolument by the establishment of the general government and who can hope for nothing there [3] the influence of some *considerable* men in office possessed of talents and popularity who partly from the same motives and partly from a desire of *playing a part* in a convulsion for their own aggrandisement will oppose the quiet adoption of the new government

[4] some considerable men out of office, from motives of ambition may be disposed to act the same part—add to these causes [5] the disinclination of the people to taxes, and of course to a strong government [6] the opposition of all men much in debt who will not wish to see a government established one object of which is to restrain the means of cheating Creditors [7] the democratical jealousy of the people which may be alarmed at the appearance of institutions that may seem calculated to place the power of the community in few hands and to raise a few individuals to stations of great pre-eminence [8] and the influence of some foreign powers who from different motives will not wish to see an energetic government established throughout the states.

[2. *The anti-Federalist version.* How the New York anti-Federalists saw themselves may be inferred from remarks made by two of their leaders, Melancton Smith and James Hughes, on two different occasions.
a. Melancton Smith. This excerpt is from a pamphlet Smith wrote in the spring of 1788 appealing to New Yorkers to elect anti-Federalist delegates. To whom did he make his appeal? (*An Address to the People of the State of New York: Showing the necessity of making amendments to the Constitution previous to its adoption* by a Plebeian [New York, 1788], in Paul L. Ford, ed., *Pamphlets on the Constitution of the United States* [Brooklyn, N.Y., 1888], pp. 109–10.)]

YOU HAVE heard that both sides on this great question agree, that there are in it [the Constitution] great defects; yet the one side tell you, choose such men as will adopt it, and then amend it—while the other say, amend previous to its adoption.—I have stated to you my reasons for the latter, and I think they are unanswerable.—Consider you the common people the yeomanry of the country, for to such I principally address myself, you are to be the principal losers, if the Constitution should prove oppressive; When a tyranny is established, there are always masters as well as slaves; the great and well-born are generally the former, and the middling classes the latter.—Attempts have been made, and will be repeated, to alarm you with the fear of consequences; but reflect there are consequences on both sides, and none can be apprehended more dreadful, than entailing on ourselves and posterity a government which will raise a few to the heights of human greatness and wealth, while it will depress the many to the extreme of poverty and wretchedness.

[b. James Hughes. As the delegates arrived at the ratifying convention at Poughkeepsie with the Federalists outnumbered forty-six to nineteen, James Hughes sent the following letter to General John Lamb, the anti-Federalist chieftain at New York City. (John Lamb Papers, New York Historical Society.)]

June 18, 1788

Dear General:
Notwithstanding the Eclat with which the Federalists left the city [New York] and the Impressions on their Mind of their Weight and

Importance, yet I believe there has not been a Time since the Revolution in which, the *Well Born*, who are the Leaders of that Party, have felt and appeared so uninfluential, as they feel and appear at this Time and Place. *How are the mighty fallen!* is an Apostrophe applicable to their desponding countenances—and ought to at least to teach their High Blown Imaginations a Lesson of Humility in future. . . .

[3. *A description of a New York City parade.* Neither Hamilton nor Smith said much about the opinions of the thirty thousand residents of New York City. There is no question that the city was overwhelmingly Federalist. The city chose Federalist convention delegates by a vote of about 2,700 to 150. In July after the news arrived that Virginia and New Hampshire had ratified, citizens paraded en masse to celebrate ratification and bring pressure on the delegates at Poughkeepsie to do likewise. The description of the parade that follows enables us to answer the question: Who in New York City supported the Constitution?

In evaluating the turnout one should keep in mind that the city had about six thousand adult men, about two-thirds of whom were "mechanics," a term used to describe craftsmen who owned their own businesses, as well as journeymen and apprentices who worked for them and common laborers. In the newspaper report that follows, the number of paraders in a particular division has been left in wherever it was given. Although the report was written by the Federalist Chairman of the Committee on Arrangements, it may be regarded as reliable. ("Federal Procession," *New York Packet*, August 5, 1788.)]

. . . About ten O'clock, 13 guns were fired from the Federal Ship, *Hamilton* being the signal for the procession to move, the different bodies of which it was composed, having already collected from their various places of meeting. It now set out from the Fields [a public park] proceeding down Broad-way to Great Dock Street, thence through Hanover Square, Queen, Chatham, Division, and Arundel streets; and from thence through Bullock street to Bayard's house in the following order. . . .

FIRST DIVISION. Foresters with axes . . . A plough drawn by six oxen . . . two men sowing grain . . . a number of gentlemen farmers . . . United States Arms supported by the Cincinnati [a society of Revolutionary War army officers] . . . a number of gardeners . . . A Band of Music. Taylors. A flag 10 by 11 feet, field sky blue, a fine landscape—Adam and Eve represented naked excepting fig leaves for aprons, nearly in full stature in a sitting posture—motto "And they sewed fig leaves together" . . . Measurers of Grain . . . Millers, Inspectors of Flour, Bakers . . . Four master bakers with the Federal loaf, 10 feet long, 27 inches in breadth, and 8 inches in height, with the names in full length of the ten states which had ratified the Constitution . . . followed by 80 masters, journeymen and apprentices with white aprons . . . Brewers . . . Distillers.

SECOND DIVISION. Coopers. Thirteen apprentice boys 13 years of age dressed in white shirts . . . forty two apprentices . . . 138 masters and journeymen . . . Butchers . . . Tanners and Curriers . . . Skinners, Breeches Makers and Glovers . . . a flag of cream colored silk . . . the coat of arms . . . motto, *"Americans encourage your own manufacturing."*

THIRD DIVISION. Cordwainers . . . the motto "Federal Cordwainers" . . . then followed the main body, 340 men.

FOURTH DIVISION. Carpenters . . . Representing under the standard of the United States a portraiture of his Excellency General Washington, the motto, "Freedom's favorite son!" . . . a motto on the frieze "The love of our country prevails" . . . the journeymen in sections, the masters in sections . . . 392 rank and file . . . Furriers . . . hatters . . . peruke makers and hairdressers . . . artificial florists . . .

FIFTH DIVISION. White Smiths . . . Cutlers . . . Confectioners . . . Stone Masons . . . Brick layers . . . 120 in number . . . Painters and Glaziers . . . Cabinet Makers . . . Windsor and Rush Chair Makers . . . 60 men with Green and Red cockades in their hats, emblematical of their business . . . the motto

> The Federal States in union bound
> O'er all the world our chairs are found

The drum makers . . . upholsterers . . . lace and fringe weavers . . . paper stainers . . . civil engineers.

SIXTH DIVISION. Black Smiths and Nailors . . . 120 in order . . . Ship joiners. Motto:

> Our Merchants may venture to ship without fear
> For Pilots of skill shall the Hamilton steer
> This federal ship will our commerce revive
> And merchants and ship wrights and joiners
> shall thrive.

Boat Builders . . . Block and pump makers . . . sail makers . . . Riggers.

SEVENTH DIVISION. The Federal Ship Hamilton, A Frigate of thirty-two guns, twenty-seven feet keel, and ten feet beam, with galleries and everything complete and in proportion, both in hull and rigging; manned with upwards of thirty seamen and marines in their different uniforms. Commanded by Commodore Nicholson, and drawn by ten horses . . . Pilots, marine society . . . masters of vessels . . . printers book binders and stationers.

EIGHTH DIVISION. Cartmen. A cart painted red with the words "Federal cart" . . . ornamented . . . and the lines

> Behold the Federal ship of fame
> The Hamilton we call her name;
> To every craft she gives employ,
> Sure cartmen have their share of joy.

Followed by 300 cartmen each wearing a laurel in his hat . . . horse doctors . . . mathematical instrument makers . . . carvers and engravers

. . . coach and coach harness makers . . . Copper smiths . . . Founders Colours . . . Tin plate workers . . . pewterers . . . Gold and Silver Smiths . . . potters, chocolate makers . . . tobacconists . . . dyers . . . brush makers . . . Tallow chandlers. A flag with 13 stripes, under these the figure of George Washington, with these words placed over him, "The Illustrious Washington, may he be the first President of the United States." At the opposite end was placed the figure of Colonel Hamilton . . . saddlers, harness and whip makers.

NINTH DIVISION. The gentlemen of the bar in their robes . . . ten students of law followed by The Philological Society . . . Columbia University . . . President and professors in their academical habits, followed by the students . . . Merchants and traders . . . preceded by the President of the Chamber of Commerce and . . . Vice President of the Bank [of New York].

TENTH DIVISION. Physicians, strangers and gentlemen, Porters.

The line of procession, containing nearly 5,000 people, and extended upwards of a mile and a half. The march was slow and majestic, and the general appearance of the scene far surpassed every one's expectations, as mere description must fall short of it. While numberless crowds were pressing on every side, the doors and windows of houses were thronged by the fair daughters of Columbia, whose animated smiles and satisfaction contributed not a little to complete the general joy . . .

The whole body having arrived at Bayard's house . . . the citizens were conducted to their several dining tables. Here they were honored by the company of Congress, of many foreigners of distinction, and the patriotic and respectable clergy of this city . . . [The tables were] calculated to accommodate 6000 persons . . .

By order of the Committee of Arrangements
Richard Platt, Chairman

As several gentlemen of some of the professions that appeared in the procession on the 23rd ult. have furnished us with complete descriptions of their respective exhibitions on that memorable day, we may, with propriety, pronounce the above account the most accurate of any, that has yet been offered to the public [—the printer].

B.

VIRGINIA

⟪In Virginia, the most wealthy, populous, and politically important southern state, a state of large plantation holders and yeoman farmers, the division of opinion was much closer than in New York. At the Philadelphia Convention, the state's delegates were split: George Washington, the presiding officer, and James Madison, the chief architect of the Constitution, were Federalists, while George Mason refused to sign the Constitution and Edmund Randolph vacillated. The chief political power in the state, Patrick Henry, refused to be a delegate because he "smelt a rat," or so it was said.

In the election of delegates to the Virginia Convention the two sides were about evenly divided, the Federalists having a slight edge, with a number of delegates, especially from the western counties, apparently undecided.

1. *The Federalist version.* a. James Madison. These accounts of his native state were sent by Madison to Thomas Jefferson, then Minister to France and his close friend and political associate. (Madison to Jefferson, December 9, 1787, and April 22, 1788, in Julian Boyd, ed., *The Papers of Thomas Jefferson* [Princeton: Princeton Univ. Press, 1955, 1956], XII, 410–11; XIII, 98–99.) Assuming that Madison's analysis is correct, how was the division in Virginia different from that of New York?]

[December 9, 1787] MY INFORMATION leads me to suppose there must be three parties in Virginia. The first for adopting without attempting amendments. This includes Genl. W[ashington] and the other deputies who signed the Constitution, Mr. Pendleton (Mr. Marshall I believe), Mr. Nicholas, Mr. Corbin, Mr. Zachy. Johnson, Col. Innis (Mr. B. Randolph as I understand), Mr. Harvey, Mr. Gabl. Jones, Docr. Jones, &c. &c. At the head of the 2d. party which urges amendments are the Governor and Mr. Mason. These do not object to the substance of the Government but contend for a few additional guards in favor of the Rights of the States and of the people. I am not able to enumerate the characters which fall in with their ideas, as distinguished from those of a third Class, at the head of which is Mr. Henry. This class concurs at present with the patrons of amendments, but will probably contend for such as strike at the essence of the System, and must lead to an adherence to the principle of the existing Confederation, which most thinking men are convinced is a visionary one, or to a partition of the Union into several Confederacies. Mr. Harrison the late Governor is with Mr. Henry. So are a number of others. The General and Admiralty Courts with most of the Bar, oppose the Constitution, but on what particular grounds I am unable to say. Genl. Nelson, Mr. Jno. Page. Col. Bland, &c. are also opponents, but on what principle and to what extent, I am equally at a loss to say. Mr. Henry is the great adversary who will render the event precarious. He is I find with his usual address, working up every possible interest, into a spirit of opposition. It is worthy of remark that whilst in Virga. and some of the other States in the middle and Southern Districts of the Union, the men of intelligence, patriotism, property, and independent circumstances, are thus divided; all of this description, with a few exceptions, in the Eastern States, and most of the middle States, are zealously attached to the proposed Constitution. In N. England, the men of letters, the principal officers of Government, the Judges and Lawyers, the Clergy, and men of property, furnish only here and there an adversary. It is not less worthy of remark that in Virginia where the mass of the people have been so much accustomed to be guided by their rulers on all new and intricate questions, they should on the present which certainly surpasses the judgment of the greater part of them, not only go before, but contrary to, their most popular leaders. And the phenomenon is the more wonderful, as a popular ground is taken by all the adversaries to the new Constitution. Perhaps the solution in both these cases, would not be very difficult; but it would lead to observations too diffusive; and to you unnecessary, I will barely observe that the case in Virga. seems to prove that the body of sober and steady people, even of the lower order, are tired of the, vicisitudes [sic], injustice and follies which have so much characterised public measures, and are impatient for some change which promises stability and repose.

[April 22, 1788] . . . The proposed Constitution still engrosses the public attention. The elections for the Convention here are but just over and promulged. From the returns (excluding those from Kentucky which are not yet known) it seems probable, though not absolutely certain that a majority of the members elect are friends to the Constitution. The superiority of abilities at least seems to lie on that side. . . .

The real sense of the people of this State cannot be easily ascertained. They are certainly attached and with warmth to a continuance of the Union; and I believe a large majority of the most intelligent and independent are equally so to the plan under consideration. On a geographical view of them, almost all the counties in the N[orthern] Neck have elected foederal deputies. The Counties on the South side of James River have pretty generally elected adversaries to the Constitution. The intermediate district is much chequered in this respect. The Counties between the blue ridge and the Alleghany have chosen friends to the Constitution without a single exception. Those Westward of the latter, have as I am informed, generally though not universally pursued the same rule. Kentucky it is supposed will be divided.

[b. George Washington. Washington sent this report of the Virginia Convention to his former comrade in arms the Marquis de Lafayette in Paris. (Washington to Lafayette, June 19, 1788, in John C. Fitzpatrick, ed., *The Writings of George Washington* [Washington, 1939], XXIX, 525.)]

IN A LETTER I wrote you a few days ago by Mr. [Joel] Barlow . . . I mentioned the accession of Maryland to the proposed government, and gave you the state of politics to that period. Since which the Convention of South Carolina has ratified the Constitution by a great majority: that of this state has been setting almost three weeks; and so nicely does it appear to be ballanced [sic] that each side asserts that it has a preponderancy of votes in its favour. . . . It is a little strange that the men of large property in the South, should be more afraid that the Constitution will produce an Aristocracy or a Monarchy, than the genuine democratical people of the East . . .

[2. *The anti-Federalist version.* Patrick Henry. As the Virginia Convention began, Patrick Henry sent the following account of Virginia opinion to John Lamb, the New York City anti-Federalist chieftain. (Henry to Lamb, June 9, 1788 in John Lamb Papers, New York Historical Society.) In what ways does Henry's account differ from Madison's and Washington's?]

I was honored by the receipt of your Favor by the hands of Col. Oswald [a messenger sent by the New York anti-Federalists], accompanying three pamphlets, for which & for the Communication resulting from a View of the whole Subject Matter, I give you sir my sincere Thanks. It is Matter of great consolation to find that the Sentiments of a vast Majority of Virginians are in Unison with those of our northern Friends. I am satisfied 4/5 of our Inhabitants are opposed to the new Scheme of Government. Indeed, in the part of this country lying south of James River, I am confident 9/10 are opposed to it.

And yet strange as it may seem, the Numbers in the Convention appear equal on both Sides; so that the Majority, which way soever it goes, will be small. The Friends & Seekers of Power, have with their usual subtilty [sic] wriggled themselves into the Choice of the people, by assuming Shapes as various as the Faces of the men they address on such Occasions. . . .

II

VIRGINIA: PATRICK HENRY vs.
JAMES MADISON

THE QUESTION OF "STATES' RIGHTS"

IN THE VIRGINIA CONVENTION PATRICK HENRY CARRIED THE DEBATE FOR the anti-Federalists—he spoke at eighteen of the twenty-three sessions and his speeches filled about a third of the record. Federalists depended primarily upon James Madison, who knew the Constitution better than any of them.

The two debaters were in many ways a strange contrast. Patrick Henry was the most formidable foe the Federalists faced anywhere. As Thomas Jefferson later said of him, "through a long and active life" he "had been the idol of his country beyond any man who ever lived." In the Revolution he "was far above all"; in fact "it is not now easy to say what we should have done without Patrick Henry." Henry had been elected Governor of the state for five terms, and his word was almost law in Virginia politics. He was a self-made man, a product of a middle-class family of the backcountry who, after failing as a storekeeper and farmer, made good as a lawyer and politician. At the age of sixty-one, in 1788, he was a prosperous plantation owner, slaveholder, and land speculator. His political strength among his backcountry supporters and aristocratic admirers lay in his unsurpassed oratory, earthy humor, and common touch. To his foes, he was an ambitious demagogue with, in Jefferson's words, "a love of money and fame." In the judgment of a recent historian he had "no clear cut program of domestic reform" but "on the balance his record is that of a liberal." (Bernard Mayo, "The Enigma of Patrick Henry," in *Myths and Men* [Athens, Ga.: Univ. of Georgia Press, 1959] pp. 17–18.) At times he was nationalistic ("I am not a Virginian; I am an American"), but by 1787 he was intransigent against the new Constitution. Some charged that he was afraid that the new government would surrender the rights of navigation on the Mississippi River to Spain and thereby jeopardize his own western land speculations. Whatever the motivation, his speeches demonstrated the flamboyant oratory for which he was famous.

James Madison was a young man; he was only thirty-seven in 1788. He was a scholar in politics who commanded attention in public councils by the depth and breadth of his learning; to Patrick Henry he was one of the "theorists and bookworms." He was born into an eminent plantation family of the Piedmont area of Virginia (between the aristocratic Tidewater and frontier backcountry), and he himself owned a small plantation and a handful of slaves. A frail and sickly youth, he was a brilliant student at Princeton, who after graduation devoted several years to study and reflection. When he entered politics about 1776 he was an admiring follower of Henry, then the radical patriot. From 1779 on he was a co-worker of Thomas Jefferson, also his senior; the two scored their greatest success in securing the separation of church and state in Virginia. Early a nationalist, he was a leader in the Continental Congress. For his work at the Philadelphia Convention, by the common acknowledgement of historians, he deserves, if any one man does, the title "father of the constitution." He helped shape its main structure of national supremacy, then in *The Federalist* essays brilliantly expounded its principles. As an orator, too, he was Henry's opposite: he pursuaded by undramatic, logical argument.

A.

A "CONSOLIDATED" OR A "MIXED" GOVERNMENT?

⟪In this first excerpt Henry and Madison debate the general character of the federal-state relationships under the Constitution. What charges does Henry make against the proposed new government? How does Madison answer them—does he admit that Henry's claims are true or does he deny them? The student will want to turn to the relevant clauses in the Constitution and ponder whose interpretation seems more valid. (Jonathan Elliot, ed., *The Debates in the Several State Conventions, on the Adoption of the Constitution,* 5 vols. [1st ed., 1836], III, 21–22, 44, 46, 53–55, 93–97.)]

Mr. Henry. Mr. Chairman, the public mind, as well as my own, is extremely uneasy at the proposed change of government. Give me leave to form one of the number of those who wish to be thoroughly acquainted with the reasons of this perilous and uneasy situation, and why we are brought hither to decide on this great national question. I consider myself as the servant of the people of this commonwealth, as a sentinel over their rights, liberty, and happiness. . . .

If a wrong step be now made, the republic may be lost forever. If this new government will not come up to the expectation of the people, and they shall be disappointed, their liberty will be lost, and tyranny must and will arise. I repeat it again, and I beg gentlemen to consider, that a wrong step, made now, will plunge us into misery, and our republic will be lost. . . . And here I would make this inquiry of those worthy characters who composed a part of the late federal Convention. I am sure they were fully impressed with the necessity of forming a great consolidated government, instead of a confederation. That this is a consolidated government is demonstrably clear; and the danger of such a government is, to my mind, very striking. I have the highest veneration for those gentlemen; but, sir, give me leave to demand, What right had they to say, *We, the people?* My political curiosity, exclusive of my anxious solicitude for the public welfare, leads me to ask, Who authorized them to speak the language of, *We, the people,* instead of, *We, the states?* States are the characteristics and the soul of a confederation. If the states be not the agents of this compact, it must be one great, consolidated, national government, of the people of all the states. . . .

The federal Convention ought to have amended the old system; for this purpose they were solely delegated; the object of their mission extended to no other consideration. You must, therefore, forgive the solicitation of one unworthy member to know what danger could have arisen under the present Confederation, and what are the causes of this proposal to change our government. . . .

If we admit this consolidated government, it will be because we like a great, splendid one. Some way or other we must be a great and mighty empire; we must have an army, and a navy, and a number of things. When the American spirit was in its youth, the language of America was different: liberty, sir, was then the primary object. We are descended from a people whose government was founded on liberty: our glorious forefathers of Great Britain made liberty the foundation of every thing. That country is become a great, mighty, and splendid nation; not because their government is strong and energetic, but, sir, because liberty is its direct end and foundation. We drew the spirit of liberty from our British ancestors: by that spirit we have triumphed over every difficulty. But now, sir, the American spirit, assisted by the ropes and chains of consolidation, is about to convert this country into a powerful and mighty empire. If you make the citizens of this country agree to become the subjects of one great consolidated empire of America, your government will not have sufficient energy to keep them together. Such a government is incompatible with the genius of republicanism. There will be no checks, no real balances, in this government. What can avail your specious, imaginary balances, your rope-dancing, chain-rattling, ridiculous ideal checks and contrivances? But, sir, we are not feared by foreigners; we do not make nations tremble. Would this constitute happiness, or secure liberty? I trust, sir, our political hemisphere will ever direct their operations to the security of those objects.

Consider our situation, sir: go to the poor man, and ask him what he does. He will inform you that he enjoys the fruits of his labor, under his own fig-tree, with his wife and children around him, in peace and security. Go to every other member of society,—you will find the same tranquil ease and content; you will find no alarms or disturbances. Why, then tell us of danger, to terrify us into an adoption of this new form of government? And yet who knows the dangers that this new system may produce? They are out of the sight of the common people: they cannot foresee latent consequences. I dread the operation of it on the middling and lower classes of people: it is for them I fear the adoption of this system. . . . I have said that I thought this a consolidated government: I will now prove it. Will the great rights of the people be secured by this government? Suppose it should prove oppressive, how can it be altered? Our bill of rights declares, "that a majority of the community hath an indubitable, unalienable, and indefeasible right to reform, alter, or abolish it, in such manner as shall be judged most conducive to the public weal."

I have just proved that one tenth, or less, of the people of America —a most despicable minority—may prevent this reform or alteration. Suppose the people of Virginia should wish to alter their government; can a majority of them do it? No; because they are connected with other men, or in other words, consolidated with other states. When the people of Virginia, at a future day, shall wish to alter their government, though they should be unanimous in this desire, yet they may be prevented therefrom by a despicable minority at the extremity of the United States. The founders of your own Constitution made your government changeable: but the power of changing it is gone from you. Whither is it gone? It is placed in the same hands that hold the rights of twelve other states; and those who hold those rights have right and power to keep them. It is not the particular government of Virginia: one of the leading features of that government is, that a majority can alter it, when necessary for the public good. This government is not a Virginian, but an American government. Is it not, therefore, a consolidated government? . . .

MR. MADISON. Give me leave to say something of the nature of the government. . . . There are a number of opinions; but the principal question is, whether it be a federal or consolidated government. In order to judge properly of the question before us, we must consider it minutely in its principal parts. I conceive myself that it is of a mixed nature; it is in a manner unprecedented; we cannot find one express example in the experience of the world. It stands by itself. In some respects it is a government of a federal nature; in others, it is of a consolidated nature. Even if we attend to the manner in which the Constitution is investigated, ratified, and made the act of the people of America, I can say, notwithstanding what the honorable gentleman has alleged, that this government is not completely consolidated, nor is it entirely federal. Who are parties to it? The people—but not the people as composing one great body; but the people as composing thirteen sovereignties. Were it, as the gentleman asserts, a consolidated government, the assent of a majority of the people would be sufficient for its establishment; and, as a majority have adopted it already, the remaining states would be bound by the act of the majority, even if they unanimously reprobated it. Were it such a government as is suggested, it would be now binding on the people of this state, without having had the privilege of deliberating upon it. But, sir, no state is bound by it, as it is, without its own consent. Should all the states adopt it, it will be then a government established by the thirteen states of America, not through the intervention of the legislatures, but by the people at large. In this particular respect, the distinction between the existing and proposed governments is very material. The existing system has been derived from the dependent derivative authority of the legislatures of the states; whereas this is derived from the superior power of the people. If we look at the manner in which alterations are to be made in it, the same idea is, in some degree, attended to. By the new system, a majority of the states cannot introduce amendments; nor are all the states required for that purpose; three fourths of them must concur in alterations; in this there is a departure from the federal idea. The members to the national House of Representatives are to be chosen by the people at large, in proportion to the numbers in the respective districts. When we come to the Senate, its members are elected by the states in their equal and political capacity. But had the government been completely consolidated, the Senate would have been chosen by the people in their individual capacity, in the same manner as the members of the other house. Thus it is of a complicated nature; and this complication, I trust, will be found to exclude the evils of absolute consolidation, as well as of a mere confederacy. If Virginia was separated from all the states, her power and authority would extend to all cases: in like manner, were all powers vested in the general government, it would be a consolidated government; but the powers of the federal government are enumerated; it can only operate in certain cases; it has legislative powers on defined and limited objects, beyond which it cannot extend its jurisdiction. . . .

But it is urged that its consolidated nature, joined to the power of direct taxation, will give it a tendency to destroy all subordinate authority; that its increasing influence will speedily enable it to absorb the state governments. I cannot think this will be the case. If the general government were wholly independent of the governments of the particular states, then indeed, usurpation might be expected to the fullest extent. But, sir, on whom does this general government depend? It derives its authority from these governments, and from the same sources from which their authority is derived. The members of the federal government are taken from the same men from whom those of the state legislatures are taken. If we consider the mode in which the federal representatives will be chosen, we shall be convinced that the general will never destroy the individual governments; and this conviction must be strengthened by an attention to the construction of the Senate. The representatives will be chosen probably under the influence of the members of the state legislatures; but there is not the least probability that the election of the latter will be influenced by the former. One hundred and sixty members represent this commonwealth in one branch of the legislature, are drawn from the people at large, and must ever possess more influence than the few men who will be elected to the general legislature.

The reasons offered on this subject, by a gentleman on the same side, (Mr. Nicholas,) were unanswerable, and have been so full that I shall add but little more on the subject. Those who wish to become federal representatives must depend on their credit with that class of men who will be the most popular in their counties, who generally represent the people in the state governments; they can, therefore, never succeed in any measure contrary to the wishes of those on whom they depend. It is almost certain, therefore, that the deliberations of the members of the federal House of Representatives will be directed to the interest of the people of America. As to the other branch, the senators will be appointed by the legislatures; and, though elected for six years, I do not conceive they will so soon forget the source from whence they derive their political existence. This election of one branch of the federal by the state legislatures, secures an absolute dependence of the former on the latter. The biennial exclusion of one third will lessen the facility of a combination, and may put a stop to intrigues. I appeal to our past experiences, whether they will attend to the interests of their constituent states. Have not those gentlemen, who have been honored with seats in Congress, *often signalized themselves by their attachment to their seats?* I wish this government may answer the expectation of its friends, and foil the apprehension of its enemies. I hope the patriotism of the people will continue, and be a sufficient guard to their liberties. I believe its tendency will be, that the state governments will counteract the general interest, and ultimately prevail. The number of the representatives is yet sufficient for our safety, and will gradually increase; and, if we consider their different sources of information, the number will not appear too small.

B.

THE POWER OF THE PURSE

❡In this excerpt Madison and Henry debate one of the key specific powers proposed for the federal government, that of taxation or what that generation called "the power of the purse." (Elliot, ed., *The Debates in the Several State Conventions, on the Adoption of the Constitution,* III, 128–29, 135–36, 147–49.)]

Mr. Madison. Mr. Chairman, in considering this great subject, I trust we shall find that part which gives the general government the power of laying and collecting taxes indispensable, and essential to the existence of any efficient or well-organized system of government: if we consult reason, and be ruled by its dictates, we shall find its justification there: if we review the experience we have had, or contemplate the history of nations, here we find ample reasons to prove its expediency. There is little reason to depend for necessary supplies on a body which is fully possessed of the power of withholding them. If a government depends on other governments for its revenues—if it must depend on the voluntary contributions of its members—its existence must be precarious. A government which relies on thirteen independent sovereignties for the means of its existence, is a solecism in theory and a mere nullity in practice. Is it consistent with reason that such a government can promote the happiness of any people? It is subversive of every principle of sound policy, to trust the safety of a community with a government totally destitute of the means of protecting itself or its members. Can Congress, after the repeated unequivocal proofs it has experienced of the utter inutility and inefficacy of requisitions, reasonably expect that they would be hereafter effectual or productive? Will not the same local interests, and other causes, militate against a compliance? Whoever hopes the contrary must ever be disappointed. The effect, sir, cannot be changed without a removal of the cause. Let each county in this commonwealth be supposed free and independent; let your revenues depend on requisitions of proportionate quotas from them; let application be made to them repeatedly:—is it to be presumed that they would comply, or that an adequate collection could be made from partial compliances? It is now difficult to collect taxes from them: how much would that difficulty be enhanced, were you to depend solely on their generosity! I appeal to the reason of every gentleman here, whether he is not persuaded that the present Confederation is as feeble as the government of Virginia would be in that case: to the same reason I appeal, whether it be compatible with prudence to continue a government of such manifest and palpable debility. . . .

I agree with the honorable gentleman (Mr. Henry) that national splendor and glory are not our objects; but does he distinguish between what will render us secure and happy at home, and what will render us respectable abroad? If we be free and happy at home, we shall be respectable abroad.

The Confederation is so notoriously feeble, that foreign nations are unwilling to form any treaties with us; they are apprized that our general government cannot perform any of its engagements, but that they may be violated at pleasure by any of the states. Our violation of treaties already entered into proves this truth unequivocally. No nation will, therefore, make any stipulations with Congress, conceding any advantages of importance to us: they will be the more averse to entering into engagements with us, as the imbecility of our government enables them to derive many advantages from our trade, without granting us any return. But were this country united by proper bands, in addition to other great advantages, we could form very beneficial treaties with foreign states. But this can never happen without a change in our system. Were we not laughed at by the minister of that nation, from which we may be able yet to extort some of the most salutary measures for this country? Were we not told that it was necessary to temporize till our government acquired consistency? Will any nation relinquish national advantages to us? You will be greatly disappointed, if you expect any such good effects from this contemptible system. Let us recollect our conduct to that country from which we have received the most friendly aid [France]. How have we dealt with that benevolent ally? Have we complied with our most sacred obligations to that nation? Have we paid the interest punctually from year to year? Is not the interest accumulating, while not a shilling is discharged of the principal? The magnanimity and forbearance of that ally are so great that she has not called upon us for her claims, even in her own distress and necessity. This, sir, is an additional motive to increase our exertions. At this moment of time a very considerable amount is due from us to that country and others.

[Here Mr. Madison mentioned the amount of the debts due to different foreign nations.]

We have been obliged to borrow money even to pay the interests of our debts. This is a ruinous and most disgraceful expedient. Is this a situation on which America can rely for security and happiness? How are we to extricate ourselves? The honorable member told us we might rely on the punctuality and friendship of the states, and that they will discharge their quotas for the future. The contributions of the states have been found inadequate from the beginning, and are diminishing instead of increasing. From the month of June, 1787, till June, 1788, they have only paid 276,641 dollars into the federal treasury for the purposes of supporting the national government, and discharging the interest of the national debts—a sum so very insufficient, that it must greatly alarm the friends of their country. Suggestions and strong assertions dissipate before these facts. I shall no longer fatigue the committee at this time, but will resume the subject as early as I can.

MR. HENRY. . . . Another gentleman tells us that no inconvenience will result from the exercise of the power of taxation by the general government; that two shillings out of ten may be saved by the impost; and that four shillings may be paid to the federal collector, and four to the state collector. A change of government will not pay money. If, from the probable amount of the imposts, you take the enormous and extravagant expenses which will certainly attend the support of this great consolidated government, I believe you will find no reduction of the public burdens by this new system. The splendid maintenance of the President, and of the members of both houses, and the salaries and fees of the swarm of officers and dependants of the government, will cost this continent immense sums. Double sets of collectors will double the expenses; to those are to be added oppressive excisemen and custom-house officers. Sir, the people have an hereditary hatred to custom-house officers. The experience of the mother country leads me to detest them. They have introduced their baneful influence into the administration, and destroyed one of the most beautiful systems that ever the world saw. Our forefathers enjoyed liberty there while that system was in its purity; but it is now contaminated by influence of every kind.

. . . Requisitions, which gentlemen affect to despise, have nothing degrading in them. On this depends our political prosperity. I never will give up that *darling* word *requisitions:* my country may give it up; a majority may wrest it from me, but I will never give it up till my grave. Requisitions are attended with one singular advantage. They are attended by deliberation. They secure to the states the benefit of correcting oppressive errors. If our Assembly thought requisitions erroneous, if they thought the demand was too great, they might at least supplicate Congress to reconsider—that it was a little too much. The power of direct taxation was called by the honorable gentleman the *soul* of the government: another gentleman called it the *lungs* of the government. We all agree that it is the most important part of the body politic. If the power of raising money be necessary for the general government, it is no less so for the states. If money be the vitals of Congress, is it not precious for those individuals from whom it is to be taken? Must I give my soul, my lungs, to Congress? Congress must have our souls; the state must have our souls. This is dishonorable and disgraceful. These two coordinate, interfering, unlimited powers of harassing the community are unexampled: it is unprecedented in history. They are the visionary projects of modern politicians. Tell me not of imaginary means, but of reality; this political solecism will never tend to the benefit of the community. It will be as oppressive in practice as it is absurd in theory. If you part from this, which the honorable gentleman tells you is the soul of Congress, you will be inevitably ruined. I tell you, they shall not have the soul of Virginia. . . .

C.

THE QUESTION OF SLAVERY

⟨In this excerpt Henry expresses his fears for one of Virginia's fundamental institutions, slavery, and Madison attempts to answer them. (Elliot, ed., *The Debates in the Several State Conventions, on the Adoption of the Constitution*, III, 453, 455–56, 589–91, 621, 623.)⟩

MR. HENRY. . . . Among ten thousand *implied powers* which they may assume, they may, if we be engaged in war, liberate every one of your slaves if they please. And this must and will be done by men, a majority of whom have no common interest with you. They will, therefore, have no feeling of your interests. It has been repeatedly said here, that the great object of a national government was national defence. That power which is said to be intended for security and safety may be rendered detestable and oppressive. If they give power to the general government to provide for the *general defence,* the means must be commensurate to the end. All the means in the possession of the people must be given to the government which is intrusted with the public defence. In this state there are two hundred and thirty-six thousand blacks, and there are many in several other states. But there are few or none in the Northern States; and yet, if the Northern States shall be of opinion that our slaves are numberless, they may call forth every national resource. May Congress not say, *that every black man* must fight? Did we not see a little of this last war? We were not so hard pushed as to make emancipation general; but acts of Assembly passed that every slave who would go to the army should be free. Another thing will contribute to bring this event about. Slavery is detested. We feel its fatal effects—we deplore it with all the pity of humanity. Let all these considerations, at some future period, press with full force on the minds of Congress. Let that urbanity, which I trust will distinguish America, and the necessity of national defence,—let all these things operate on their minds; they will search that paper, and see if they have power of manumission. And have they not, sir? Have they not power to provide for the general defence and welfare? May they not think that these call for the abolition of slavery? May they not pronounce all slaves free, and will they not be warranted by that power? This is no ambiguous implication or logical deduction. The paper speaks to the point: they have the power in clear, unequivocal terms, and will clearly and certainly exercise it. As much as I deplore slavery, I see that prudence forbids its abolition. I deny that the general government ought to set them free, because a decided majority of the states have not the ties of sympathy and fellow-feeling for those whose interest would be affected by their emancipation. The majority of Congress is to the north, and the slaves are to the south.

In this situation, I see a great deal of the property of the people of Virginia in jeopardy, and their peace and tranquillity gone. I repeat it again, that it would rejoice my very soul that every one of my fellow-beings was emancipated. As we ought with gratitude to admire that decree of Heaven which has numbered us among the free, we ought to lament and deplore the necessity of holding our fellowmen in bondage. But is it practicable, by any human means, to liberate them without producing the most dreadful and ruinous consequences? We ought to possess them in the manner we inherited them from our ancestors, as their manumission is incompatible with the felicity of our country. But we ought to soften, as much as possible, the rigor of their unhappy fate. I know that, in a variety of particular instances, the legislature, listening to complaints, have admitted their emancipation. Let me not dwell on this subject. I will only add that this, as well as every other property of the people of Virginia, is in jeopardy, and put in the hands of those who have no similarity of situation with us. This is a local matter, and I can see no propriety in subjecting it to Congress. . . .

Mr. MADISON. . . . I was struck with surprise when I heard him express himself alarmed with respect to the emancipation of slaves. Let me ask, if they should even attempt it, if it will not be a usurpation of power. There is no power to warrant it, in that paper. If there be, I know it not. But why should it be done? Says the honorable gentleman, for the general welfare: it will infuse strength into our system. Can any member of this committee suppose that it will increase our strength? Can any one believe that the American councils will come into a measure which will strip them of their property, and discourage and alienate the affections of five thirteenths of the Union? Why was nothing of this sort aimed at before? I believe such an idea never entered into any American breast, nor do I believe it ever will enter into the heads of those gentlemen who substitute unsupported suspicions for reasons. . . .

Mr. HENRY. . . . He asked me where was the power of emancipating slaves. I say it will be implied, unless implication be prohibited. He admits that the power of granting passports will be in the new Congress without the insertion of this restriction; yet he can show me nothing like such a power granted in that Constitution. Notwithstanding he admits their right to this power by implication, he says that I am unfair and uncandid in my deduction that they can emancipate our slaves, though the word *emancipation* is not mentioned in it. They can exercise power by implication in one instance, as well as in another. Thus, by the gentleman's own argument, they can exercise the power, though it be not delegated. . . .

NEW YORK: ALEXANDER HAMILTON vs.
MELANCTON SMITH

THE QUESTION OF "DEMOCRACY"

WHILE MADISON AND HENRY WERE EXCHANGING BARBS, ALEXANDER HAMilton and Melancton Smith debated in the New York convention at Poughkeepsie. But there, the debate, unlike that in Virginia, "began with, and rarely departed from, some underlying sentiment that what was at stake was the question of rich against poor, aristocrat against 'common man.' " (George Dangerfield, *Chancellor Robert R. Livingston of New York, 1746–1813* [New York, Harcourt, Brace & Company, 1960], p. 226.)

Hamilton and Smith in many ways symbolized the two sides they represented. Hamilton's career was a spectacular American success story. An illegitimate child of a ne'er-do-well West Indies Scotsman, he was sent to Columbia College by a patron, then made a brilliant career in the army as a staff officer at Washington's headquarters, where he was close to the commander-in-chief. He married the daughter of General Philip Schuyler, a powerful landlord of the Hudson Valley, whose other son-in-law was Stephen Van Rensselaer, owner of perhaps the largest tenanted estate of New York. Hamilton's leading co-workers at the convention were Chancellor Robert R. Livingston, another rich landowner, and John Jay, who had married into another branch of the Livingston family. These were the "well born" to whom the anti-Federalists referred. Hamilton himself was not wealthy. He made his living as a lawyer, drawing clients from business circles of New York City and Albany. He was strongly nationalistic, especially as a result of his wartime experiences with the weaknesses of the central government. But his proposals at the Philadelphia Convention were for a government too centralized and too aristocratic to be considered seriously. His plan called for a President and Senate elected for life, a House elected by the people every two years, and a President with the power to appoint state governors and veto state laws. Despite his misgivings about the final product he campaigned ardently for the Constitution, writing about half of *The Federalist* essays. At the New York ratifying convention the short, dapper military figure argued in a style that was eloquent and dramatic.

That Melancton Smith, Hamilton's leading opponent, is not better known is typical of his party. He was not affiliated with one of the established landed or commercial families of the state. The son of a yeoman farmer, he was self-educated and self-made. Starting very likely as a clerk in a Poughkeepsie store he was a successful merchant and farmer who became well-to-do during the Revolution as an army contractor and speculator in land. In the Revolution he was a militia captain, then the sheriff of Dutchess County (replacing a Livingston), and county judge. The highest office he held was as a member of the Articles of Confederation congress. He was a close political advisor to Governor Clinton and perhaps the best pamphleteer and strategist in the anti-Federalist camp. Although he had moved to New York City after the Revolution, he had to be elected to the ratifying convention in 1788 from his former home county, Dutchess, safe anti-Federalist territory. Contemporaries described Smith as "a man of rough exterior, powerful in bodily appearance and undaunted in expressing his mind" and described his oratory as "plain, dry and syllogistic," a far cry from that of his Virginia counterpart, Patrick Henry.

A.

HOW MANY REPRESENTATIVES IN THE HOUSE?

⟨In New York the anti-Federalists went over the Constitution systematically, beginning with Article I, Section 2, Clause 3, which provided that the "number of representatives shall not exceed one for every thirty thousand persons." Smith challenged this clause, and Hamilton defended it. What were Smith's objections? What was Hamilton's defense? (Elliot, ed., *The Debates in the Several State Conventions, on the Adoption of the Constitution*, II, 226–30, 238–39.)⟩

MR. SMITH. He would now proceed to state his objections to the clause just read, (section 2, of article 1, clause 3.) His objections were comprised under three heads: 1st, the rule of apportionment is unjust; 2d, there is no precise number fixed on, below which the house shall not be reduced; 3d, it is inadequate.

In the first place, the rule of apportionment of the representatives is to be according to the whole number of white inhabitants, with three fifths of all others; that is, in plain English, each state is to send representatives in proportion to the number of freemen, and three fifths of the slaves it contains. He could not see any rule by which slaves were to be included in the ratio of representation. The principle of a representation being that every free agent should be concerned in governing himself, it was absurd in giving that power to a man who could not exercise it. Slaves have no will of their own. The very operation of it was to give certain privileges to those people who were so wicked as to keep slaves. He knew it would be admitted that this rule of apportionment was founded on unjust principles, but that it was the result of accommodation; which, he supposed, we should be under the necessity of admitting, if we meant to be in union with the Southern States, though utterly repugnant to his feelings.

In the second place, the number was not fixed by the Constitution, but left at the discretion of the legislature; perhaps he was mistaken; it was his wish to be informed. He understood, from the Constitution, that sixty-five members were to compose the House of Representatives for three years; that after that time, the census was to be taken, and the numbers to be ascertained by the legislature, on the following principles: 1st, they shall be apportioned to the respective states according to numbers; 2d, each state shall have one, at least; 3d, they shall never exceed one to every thirty thousand. If this was the case, the first Congress that met might reduce the number below what it now is—a power inconsistent with every principle of a free government, to leave it to the discretion of the rulers to determine the number of representatives of the people. There was no kind of security except in the integrity of the men who were intrusted; and if you have no other security, it is idle to contend about constitutions.

In the third place, supposing Congress should declare that there should be one representative for every thirty thousand of the people, in his opinion, it would be incompetent to the great purposes of representation. It was, he said, the fundamental principle of a free government, that the people should make the laws by which they were to be governed. He who is controlled by another is a slave; and that government which is directed by the will of any one, or a few, or any number less than is the will of the community, is a government for slaves.

The new point was, How was the will of the community to be expressed? It was not possible for them to come together; the multitude would be too great: in order, therefore, to provide against this inconvenience, the scheme of representation had been adopted, by which the people deputed others to represent them. Individuals entering into society became one body, and that body ought to be animated by one mind; and he conceived that every form of government should have that complexion. It was true, notwithstanding all the experience we had from others, it had appeared that the experiment of representation had been fairly tried; there was something like it in the ancient republics, in which, being of small extent, the people could easily meet together, though, instead of deliberating, they only considered of those things which were submitted to them by their magistrates. In Great Britain, representation had been carried much further than in any government we knew of, except our own; but in that country it now had only a name. America was the only country in which the first fair opportunity had been offered. When we were colonies, our representation was better than any that was then known: since the revolution, we had advanced still nearer to perfection. He considered it as an object, of all others the most important, to have it fixed on its true principle; yet he was convinced that it was impracticable to have such a representation in a consolidated government. However, said he, we may approach a great way towards perfection by increasing the representation and limiting the powers of Congress. He considered that the great interests and liberties of the people could only be secured by the state governments. He admitted that, if the new government was only confined to great national objects, it would be less exceptionable; but it extended to every thing dear to human nature. That this was the case, would be proved without any long chain of reasoning; for that power which had both the purse and the sword had the government of the whole country, and might extend its powers to any and to every object. He had already observed that, by the true doctrine of representation, this principle was established—that the representative must be chosen by the free will of the majority of his constituents. It therefore followed that the representative should be chosen from small districts. This being admitted, he would ask, Could 65 men for 3,000,000, or 1 for 30,000, be chosen in this manner? Would they be possessed of the requisite information to make happy the great number of souls that were spread over this extensive country? . . .

He said, he would pursue these observations no further at present,— and concluded with making the following motion:

"*Resolved*, That it is proper that the number of representatives be fixed at the rate of one for every twenty thousand inhabitants, to be ascertained on the principles mentioned in the 2d section of the 1st article of the Constitution, until they amount to three hundred; after which they shall be apportioned among the states, in proportion to the number of inhabitants of the states respectively; and that, before the first enumeration shall be made, the several states shall be entitled to choose double the number of representatives, for that purpose mentioned in the Constitution."

Mr. Hamilton. . . . I now proceed to consider the objection with regard to the number of representatives, as it now stands. I am persuaded the system, in this respect, stands on a better footing than the gentlemen imagine.

It has been asserted that it will be in the power of Congress to reduce the number. I acknowledge that there are no direct words of prohibition, but contend that the true and genuine construction of the clause gives Congress no power whatever to reduce the representation below the number as it now stands. Although they may limit, they can never diminish the number. One representative for every thirty thousand inhabitants is fixed as the standard of increase; till, by the natural course of population, it shall become necessary to limit the ratio. Probably, at present, were this standard to be immediately applied, the representation would considerably exceed sixty-five. In three years, it would exceed one hundred. If I understand the gentlemen, they contend that the number may be enlarged, or may not. I admit that this is in the discretion of Congress; and I submit to the committee whether it be not necessary and proper. Still, I insist that an immediate limitation is not probable, nor was it in the contemplation of the Convention. But, sir, who will presume to say to what precise point the representation ought to be increased? This is a matter of opinion, and opinions are vastly different upon the subject. A proof of this is drawn from the representations in the state legislatures. In Massachusetts, the Assembly consists of about three hundred; in South Carolina, of nearly one hundred; in New York, there are sixty-five. It is observed generally that the number ought to be large; let the gentlemen produce their criterion. I confess it is difficult for me to say what number may be said to be sufficiently large. On one hand, it ought to be considered that a small number will act with more facility, system, and decision; on the other, that a large one may enhance the difficulty of corruption. The Congress is to consist, at first, of ninety-one members. This, to a reasonable man, may appear as near the proper medium as any number whatever, at least for the present. There is one source of increase, also, which does not depend upon any constructions of the Constitution; it is the creation of new states. Vermont, Kentucky, and Franklin, [now Tennessee] will probably become independent. New members of the Union will also be formed from the unsettled tracts of western territory.

These must be represented, and will all contribute to swell the federal legislature. If the whole number in the United States be, at present, three millions, as is commonly supposed, according to the ratio of one for thirty thousand, we shall have, on the first census, a hundred representatives. In ten years, thirty more will be added; and in twenty-five years, the number will be double. Then, sir, we shall have two hundred, if the increase goes on in the same proportion. The Convention of Massachusetts, who made the same objections, have fixed upon this number as the point to which they chose to limit the representation. But can we pronounce, with certainty, that it will not be expedient to go beyond this number? We cannot. Experience alone must determine. This matter may, with more safety, be left to the discretion of the legislature, as it will be the interest of the large and increasing states of Massachusetts, New York, Pennsylvania, &c., to augment the representation. Only Connecticut, Rhode Island, Delaware, and Maryland, can be interested in limiting it. We may, therefore, safely calculate upon a growing representation, according to the advance of population, and the circumstances of the country. The state governments possess inherent advantages, which will ever give them an influence and ascendency over the national government, and will forever preclude the possibility of federal encroachments. That their liberties, indeed, can be subverted by the federal head, is repugnant to every rule of political calculation. Is not this arrangement, then, sir, a most wise and prudent one? Is not the present representation fully adequate to our present exigencies, and sufficient to answer all the purposes of the Union? I am persuaded that an examination of the objects of the federal government will afford a conclusive answer.

Many other observations might be made on this subject, but I cannot now pursue them; for I feel myself not a little exhausted. I beg leave, therefore, to waive, for the present, the further discussion of the question.

B.

RULE BY THE "MIDDLING CLASSES" OR THE "ARISTOCRACY"?

⟪On the following day Smith and Hamilton renewed their debate, broadening the argument to reveal their respective philosophies of government. How far apart were they? Were their differences fundamental? (Elliot, ed., *The Debates in the Several State Conventions, on the Adoption of the Constitution*, II, 245–48, 251–60.)⟫

MR. SMITH. I had the honor, yesterday, of submitting an amendment to the clause under consideration, with some observations in support of it. I hope I shall be indulged in making some additional remarks in reply to what has been offered by the honorable gentleman from New York [Mr. Hamilton]. . . .

To determine whether the number of representatives proposed by this Constitution is sufficient, it is proper to examine the qualifications which this house ought to possess, in order to exercise their power discreetly for the happiness of the people. The idea that naturally suggests itself to our minds, when we speak of representatives, is, that they resemble those they represent. They should be a true picture of the people, possess a knowledge of their circumstances and their wants, sympathize in all their distresses, and be disposed to seek their true interests. The knowledge necessary for the representative of a free people not only comprehends extensive political and commercial information, such as is acquired by men of refined education, who have leisure to attain to high degrees of improvement, but it should also comprehend that kind of acquaintance with the common concerns and occupations of the people, which men of the middling class of life, are, in general, more competent to than those of a superior class. To understand the true commercial interests of a country, not only requires just ideas of the general commerce of the world, but also, and principally, a knowledge of the productions of your own country, and their value, what your soil is capable of producing, the nature of your manufactures, and the capacity of the country to increase both. To exercise the power of laying taxes, duties, and excises, with discretion, requires something more than an acquaintance with the abstruse parts of the system of finance. It calls for a knowledge of the circumstances and ability of the people in general—a discernment how the burdens imposed will bear upon the different classes.

From these observations results this conclusion—that the number of representatives should be so large, as that, while it embraces the men of the first class, it should admit those of the middling class of life. I am convinced that this government is so constituted that the representatives will generally be composed of the first class in the community, which I shall distinguish by the name of the *natural aristocracy* of the country. I do not mean to give offence by using this term. I am sensible this idea is treated by many gentlemen as chimerical. I shall be asked what is meant by the *natural aristocracy*, and told that no such distinction of classes of men exists among us. It is true, it is our singular felicity that we have no legal or hereditary distinctions of this kind; but still there are real differences. Every society naturally divides itself into classes. The Author of nature has bestowed on some greater capacities than others; birth, education, talents, and wealth, create distinctions among men as visible, and of as much influence, as titles, stars, and garters. In every society, men of this class will command a superior degree of respect; and if the government is so constituted as to admit but few to exercise the powers of it, it will, according to the natural course of things, be in their hands. Men in the middling class, who are qualified as representatives, will not be so anxious to be chosen as those of the first. When the number is so small, the office will be highly elevated and distinguished; the style in which the members live will probably be high; circumstances of this kind will render the place of a representative not a desirable one to sensible, substantial men, who have been used to walk in the plain and frugal paths of life.

Besides, the influence of the great will generally enable them to succeed in elections. It will be difficult to combine a district of country containing thirty or forty thousand inhabitants,—frame your election laws as you please,—in any other character, unless it be in one of conspicuous military, popular, civil, or legal talents. The great easily form associations; the poor and middling class form them with difficulty. If the elections be by plurality,—as probably will be the case in this state, —it is almost certain none but the great will be chosen, for they easily unite their interests: the common people will divide, and their divisions will be promoted by the others. There will be scarcely a chance of their uniting in any other but some great man, unless in some popular demagogue, who will probably be destitute of principle. A substantial yeoman, of sense and discernment, will hardly ever be chosen. From these remarks, it appears that the government will fall into the hands of the few and the great. This will be a government of oppression. I do not mean to declaim against the great, and charge them indiscriminately with want of principle and honesty. The same passions and prejudices govern all men. The circumstances in which men are placed in a great measure give a cast to the human character. Those in middling circumstances have less temptation; they are inclined by habit, and the company with whom they associate, to set bounds to their passions and appetites. If this is not sufficient, the want of means to gratify them will be a restraint: they are obliged to employ their time in their respective callings; hence the substantial yeomanry of the country are more temperate, of better morals, and less ambition, than the great. The latter do not feel for the poor and middling class; the reasons are obvious—they are not obliged to use the same pains and labor to procure property as the other. They feel not the inconveniences arising from the payment of small sums. The great consider themselves above the common people, entitled to more respect, do not associate with them; they fancy themselves to have a right of preeminence in every thing.

In short, they possess the same feelings, and are under the influence of the same motives, as an hereditary nobility. I know the idea that such a distinction exists in this country is ridiculed by some; but I am not the less apprehensive of danger from their influence on this account. Such distinctions exist all the world over, have been taken notice of by all writers on free government, and are founded in the nature of things. It has been the principal care of free governments to guard against the encroachments of the great. Common observation and experience prove the existence of such distinctions. Will any one say that there does not exist in this country the pride of family, of wealth, of talents, and that they do not command influence and respect among the common people? Congress, in their address to the inhabitants of the province of Quebec, in 1775, state this distinction in the following forcible words, quoted from the Marquis Beccaria: "In every human society there is an essay continually tending to confer on one part the height of power and happiness, and to reduce the other to the extreme of weakness and misery. The intent of good laws is to oppose this effort, and to diffuse their influence universally and equally." We ought to guard against the government being placed in the hands of this class. They cannot have that sympathy with their constituents which is necessary to connect them closely to their interests. Being in the habit of profuse living, they will be profuse in the public expenses. They find no difficulty in paying their taxes, and therefore do not feel public burdens. Besides if they govern, they will enjoy the emoluments of the government. The middling class, from their frugal habits, and feeling themselves the public burdens, will be careful how they increase them.

But I may be asked, Would you exclude the first class in the community from any share in legislation? I answer, By no means. They would be factious, discontented, and constantly disturbing the government. It would also be unjust. They have their liberties to protect, as well as others, and the largest share of property. But my idea is, that the Constitution should be so framed as to admit this class, together with a sufficient number of the middling class to control them. You will then combine the abilities and honesty of the community, a proper degree of information, and a disposition to pursue the public good. A representative body, composed principally of respectable yeomanry, is the best possible security to liberty. When the interest of this part of the community is pursued, the public good is pursued, because the body of every nation consists of this class, and because the interest of both the rich and the poor are involved in that of the middling class. No burden can be laid on the poor but what will sensibly affect the middling class. Any law rendering property insecure would be injurious to them. When, therefore, this class in society pursue their own interest, they promote that of the public, for it is involved in it.

Mr. Hamilton then resumed his argument. . . . Sir, no man agrees more perfectly than myself to the main principle for which the gentlemen contend. I agree that there should be a broad democratic branch in the national legislature. But this matter sir, depends on circumstances. It is impossible, in the first instance, to be precise and exact with regard to the number; and it is equally impossible to determine to what point it may be proper in future to increase it. On this ground I am disposed to acquiesce. In my reasonings on this subject of government, I rely more on the interests and opinions of men, than on any speculative parchment provisions whatever. I have found that constitutions are more or less excellent as they are more or less agreeable to the natural operation of things. I am, therefore, disposed not to dwell long on curious speculations, or pay much attention to modes and forms; but to adopt a system whose principles have been sanctioned by experience, adapt it to the real state of our country, and depend on probable reasonings for its operation and result. I contend that sixty-five and twenty-six, in two bodies, afford perfect security, in the present state of things; and that the regular progressive enlargement, which was in the contemplation of the general Convention, will leave not an apprehension of danger in the most timid and suspicious mind. It will be the interest of the large states to increase the representation. This will be the standing instruction to their delegates. But, say the gentlemen, the members of Congress will be interested not to increase the number, as it will diminish their relative influence. In all their reasoning upon this subject, there seems to be this fallacy: They suppose that the representative will have no motive of action, on the one side, but a sense of duty; or on the other, but corruption. They do not reflect that he is to return to the community; that he is dependent on the will of the people, and that it cannot be his interest to oppose their wishes. Sir, the general sense of the people will regulate the conduct of their representatives. I admit that there are exceptions to this rule: there are certain conjectures, when it may be necessary and proper to disregard the opinions which the majority of the people have formed. But, in the general course of things, the popular views, and even prejudices, will direct the actions of the rulers.

All governments, even the most despotic, depend, in a great degree, on opinion. In free republics, it is most peculiarly the case. In these, the will of the people makes the essential principle of the government; and the laws which control the community receive their tone and spirit from the public wishes. It is the fortunate situation of our country, that the minds of the people are exceedingly enlightened and refined. Here, then, we may expect the laws to be proportionably agreeable to the standard of perfect policy, and the wisdom of public measures to consist with the most intimate conformity between the views of the representative and his constituent. If the general voice of the people be for an increase, it undoubtedly must take place. They have it in their power to instruct their representatives; and the state legislatures, which appoint the senators, may enjoin it also upon them. Sir, if I believed that the number would remain at sixty-five, I confess I should give my vote for an amendment, though in a different form from the one proposed.

The amendment proposes a ratio of one for twenty thousand. I would ask by what rule of reasoning it is determined that one man is a better representative for twenty than thirty thousand. . . . Besides, the President of the United States will be himself the representative of the people. From the competition that ever subsists between the branches of government, the President will be induced to protect their rights, whenever they are invaded by either branch. On whatever side we view this subject, we discover various and powerful checks to the encroachments of Congress. The true and permanent interests of the members are opposed to corruption. Their number is vastly too large for easy combination. The rivalship between the houses will forever prove an insuperable obstacle. The people have an obvious and powerful protection in their state governments. Should any thing dangerous be attempted, these bodies of perpetual observation will be capable of forming and conducting plans of regular opposition. Can we suppose the people's love of liberty will not, under the incitement of their legislative leaders be roused into resistance, and the madness of tyranny be extinguished at a blow? Sir, the danger is too distant; it is beyond all rational calculations.

It has been observed, by an honorable gentleman, that pure democracy, if it were practicable, would be the most perfect government. Experience has proved that no position in politics is more false than this. The ancient democracies, in which the people themselves deliberated, never possessed one feature of good government. Their very character was tyranny; their figure, deformity. When they assembled, the field of debate presented an ungovernable mob, not only incapable of deliberation, but prepared for every enormity. In these assemblies, the enemies of the people brought forward their plans of ambition systematically. They were opposed by their enemies of another party; and it became a matter of contingency, whether the people subjected themselves to be led blindly by one tyrant or by another.

It was remarked yesterday, that a numerous representation was necessary to obtain the confidence of the people. This is not generally true. The confidence of the people will easily be gained by a good administration. This is the true touchstone. I could illustrate the position by a variety of historical examples, both ancient and modern. . . .

It has been further, by the gentlemen in the opposition, observed, that a large representation is necessary to understand the interests of the people. This principle is by no means true in the extent to which the gentlemen seem to carry it. I would ask, Why may not a man understand the interests of thirty as well as of twenty? The position appears to be made upon the unfounded presumption that all the interests of all parts of the community must be represented. No idea is more erroneous than this. Only such interests are proper to be represented as are involved in the powers of the general government. These interests come completely under the observation of one or a few men; and the requisite information is by no means augmented in proportion to the increase of number. What are the objects of the government? Commerce, taxation, &c. In order to comprehend the interests of commerce, is it necessary to know how wheat is raised, and in what proportion it is produced in one district and in another? By no means. Neither is this species of knowledge necessary in general calculations upon the subject of taxation. The information necessary for these purposes is that which is open to every intelligent inquirer, and of which five men may be as perfectly possessed as fifty. In royal governments, there are usually particular men to whom the business of taxation is committed. These men have the forming of systems of finance, and the regulation of the revenue. I do not mean to commend this practice. It proves, however, this point—that a few individuals may be competent to these objects, and that large numbers are not necessary to perfection in the science of taxation. But grant, for a moment, that this minute and local knowledge the gentlemen contend for is necessary; let us see if, under the new Constitution, it will not probably be found in the representation. The natural and proper mode of holding elections will be, to divide the state into districts, in proportion to the number to be elected. This state will consequently be divided, at first, into six. One man from each district will probably possess all the knowledge gentlemen can desire. Are the senators of this state more ignorant of the interests of the people than the Assembly? Have they not ever enjoyed their confidence as much? Yet, instead of six districts, they are elected in four; and the chance of their being collected from the smaller divisions of the state consequently diminishes. Their number is but twenty-four; and their powers are co-extensive with those of the Assembly, and reach objects which are most dear to the people—life, liberty, and property.

Sir, we hear constantly a great deal which is rather calculated to awake our passions, and create prejudices, than to conduct us to the truth, and teach us our real interests. I do not suppose this to be the design of the gentlemen. Why, then are we told so often of an aristocracy? For my part, I hardly know the meaning of this word, as it is applied. If all we hear be true, this government is really a very bad one. But who are the aristocracy among us? Where do we find men elevated to a perpetual rank above their fellow-citizens, and possessing powers entirely independent of them? The arguments of the gentlemen only go to prove that there are men who are rich, men who are poor, some who are wise, and others who are not; that, indeed, every distinguished man is an aristocrat. This reminds me of a description of the aristocrats I have seen in a late publication styled the Federal Farmer. The author reckons in the aristocracy all governors of states, members of Congress, chief magistrates, and all officers of the militia. This description, I presume to say, is ridiculous. The image is a phantom. Does the new government render a rich man more eligible than a poor one? No. It requires no such qualification. It is bottomed on the broad and equal principle of your state constitution.

Sir, if the people have it in their option to elect their most meritorious men, is this to be considered as an objection? Shall the Constitution oppose their wishes, and abridge their most invaluable privilege? While property continues to be pretty equally divided, and a considerable share of information pervades the community, the tendency of the people's suffrages will be to elevate merit even from obscurity. As riches increase and accumulate in few hands, as luxury prevails in society, virtue will be in a greater degree considered as only a graceful appendage of wealth, and the tendency of things will be to depart from the republican standard. This is the real disposition of human nature: it is what neither the honorable member nor myself can correct; it is a common misfortune, that awaits our state constitution as well as all others.

The Hon. MELANCTON SMITH rose, and observed, that the gentleman might have spared many of his remarks in answer to the ideas he had advanced. The only way to remedy and correct the faults in the proposed Constitution was, he imagined, to increase the representation and limit the powers. He admitted that no precise number could be fixed upon. His object only was to augment the number in such a degree as to render the government more favorable to liberty. The gentleman had charged his argument, that it would be the interest of Congress to diminish the number of representatives, as being puerile. It was only made in answer to another of the gentleman's, which he thought equally weak—that it would be their interest to increase it. It appeared to him, he said, evident that the relative interests of the states would not be in the least degree increased by augmenting the numbers. The honorable member had assured the committee that the states would be checks upon the general government, and had pledged himself to point out and demonstrate the operation of these checks. For his own part, he could see no possibility of checking a government of independent powers, which extended to all objects and resources without limitation. What he lamented was, that no constitutional checks were provided—such checks as would not leave the exercise of government to the operation of causes which, in their nature, are variable and uncertain. . . .

The gentleman, continued Mr. Smith, had ridiculed his idea of an aristocracy, and had entered into a definition of the word. He himself agreed to this definition, but the dispute was not of words, but things. He was convinced that in every society there were certain men exalted above the rest. These men he did not consider as destitute of morality or virtue. He only insisted that they could not feel sympathetically the wants of the people.

THE ANTI-FEDERALISTS DIVIDE

THE QUESTION OF AMENDMENTS

It was one thing to weigh the merits of the Federalist arguments for the Constitution and the anti-Federalist arguments against it. It was another thing to decide the more difficult problem of voting at the final showdown. Federalists remained united, but anti-Federalists divided. In Virginia Patrick Henry obstinately voted against the Constitution to the very end. But in New York Melancton Smith voted for it, bringing over enough anti-Federalists to have the convention ratify by a vote of thirty to twenty-seven and leaving the intransigent anti-Federalists—for whom Abraham Yates will speak—bitter over the results. To understand the division between the "adopting" and "non-adopting" anti-Federalists, as they were then called, the reader now will have to examine Smith's reasons for voting for adoption, the amendments anti-Federalists wanted, and Yates's criticism.

A.

MELANCTON SMITH VOTES FOR RATIFICATION

⟨From the beginning of the convention, although the anti-Federalists outnumbered the Federalists more than two to one, they were divided as to the tactics they should pursue. Some wanted to reject the Constitution completely. Most wanted to amend it, but how to get the amendments—there was the rub. The dominant view at first was that the Constitution should be amended prior to its adoption by a second constitutional convention. At first most anti-Federalists were willing to ratify only *on condition* that amendments were guaranteed. When the news arrived that New Hampshire, the ninth state, had ratified, thus putting the new Constitution into effect, the question confronting the anti-Federalists began to change: Should New York be inside or outside the union?

1. *Melancton Smith's Goals.* In the following letter to a political friend Smith explains his goals and his problems. What were they?

(Smith to Nathan Dane, June 28, 1788, in E. C. Burnet, ed., *Letters of the Members of Continental Congress*, 8 vols. [Washington, 1921–38], VIII, corrected against the original in Dane Manuscripts, Beverly Historical Society, Mass.)]

DEAR SIR:

I am favored with yours of the 24th Inst. The accession of New Hampshire will have no other effect upon our convention, than softning [*sic*] them to consider what is proper to be done, in the present situation of things, if it has that—Indeed I can scarcely perceive any effect it has had—And the most I fear is that there will not be a sufficient degree of moderation in some of our most influential men, calmly to consider the circumstances in which we are, and to accommodate our decision, to these circumstances.

You have had too much experience in public life not to know, that pride, passion, and interested motives have great influence in all public bodies—They no doubt have their influence in this—From my own situation, perhaps, more than from any better principle, I feel none of these, except, it is probable, a wish to support the party with whom I am connected as far as is consistent with propriety. But, I know, my great object is, to procure such amendments in this government, as to prevent its attaining the ends, for which it appears to me, and to you calculated—I am therefore very anxious to procure good amendments—I had rather recommend substantial amendments, than adopt it conditionally with unimportant ones, leaving our critical situation out of the question.

I do not find these endeavors sufficiently seconded—The principal labor of managing the Controversy lies upon me—Hitherto the amendments proposed are substantial, they will continue so—but as no question is taken on any, it is questionable whether, the most important will not be yielded, under the Idea of making previous conditional amendments—When I am persuaded, if we can agree, to make the condition, a subsequent one, that is, to take place in one or two years after adoption or the ratification to become void, we can accommodate with the advocates of the constitution for more substantial amendments.

[2. *Melancton Smith's Explanation.* In the weeks that followed Smith's letter the news arrived that Virginia had also ratified, leaving New York the only important holdout. To force the issue farther, Federalists threatened that, if the convention did not ratify, New York's southern counties would secede and join the union. Against this background and amidst complicated maneuvers, Smith led the move to abandon the conditional ratification and to ratify *in full confidence* that amendments would be made. In a caucus of anti-Federalist delegates, the "violent members" were "much enraged," and, according to one observer, "some detest Smith as much as Hamilton." A few months later, these "non-adopting" anti-Federalists blocked the choice of Smith as New York's first United States Senator.

In the following speech to the convention, Smith offers a public explanation of his action. Because the official recorder left the convention in the closing weeks, this version of his speech is from a newspaper report. ("Copy of a letter from a Gentleman in Poughkeepsie" in *New York Daily Advertiser*, July 28, 1788.) What were the reasons Smith gave?]

ON WEDNESDAY [July 23rd] the Convention finished the consideration of the amendments, and took up the proposition of adopting the Constitution with three conditions annexed. Mr. [Samuel] Jones moved to insert the words in full confidence, instead of the words upon condition [that the amendments be adopted]. Mr. M. Smith rose and declared his determination to vote against a condition. He urged that however it might otherwise be presumed he was consistent in his principles and conduct. He was as thoroughly convinced then as he ever had been, that the Constitution was radically defective—amendments to it had always been the object of his pursuit, and until Virginia came in, he had reason to believe they might have been obtained previous to the operation of the Government. He was now satisfied they could not, and it was equally the dictate of reason and duty to quit his first ground, and advance so far as that they might be received into the union. He should hereafter pursue his important and favorite object of amendments, with equal zeal as before, but in a practicable way; which was only in the mode prescribed by the Constitution.

On the first suggestion of the plan then under consideration, he thought it might have answered the purpose; but from the reasonings of gentlemen in opposition to it, and whose opinions alone would deservedly have vast weight in the national councils, as well as from the sentiments of persons abroad, he was now persuaded the proposition would not be received, however doubtful it might appear, considered merely as an abstract and speculative question. The thing must now be abandoned as fallacious, for if persisted in, it would certainly prove in the event, only a dreadful deception to those who were serious for joining the Union.

He then placed in a striking and affecting light, the situation of this State in case we should not be received by Congress. Convulsions in the Southern part, factions and discord in the rest. The strength of his own party, who were seriously anxious for amending the Government, would be dissipated; their union lost—their object probably defeated—and they would, to use the simple figurative language of scripture, be dispersed like sheep on a mountain. He therefore concluded that it was no more than a proper discharge of his public duty, as well as the most advisable way of obtaining the great end of his opposition, to vote against any proposition which would not be received as a ratification of the Constitution.

B.

THE AMENDMENTS ANTI-FEDERALISTS WANTED

❡What were the "substantial amendments" Smith wanted? Taken together they enable us to see the kind of government the anti-Federalists would have constructed if they had had the power. Amendments like these were proposed in other state conventions; New York's were only a little more extreme than others. In the "preamble" the reader will want to compare the protections proposed for individual liberties to those incorporated in the Bill of Rights in 1791. The amendments in the heart of the document propose changes in the structure of the government which should be compared to the relevant sections of the Constitution. How would the anti-Federalists have changed the legislative, executive, and judicial branches of the federal government? How would they have changed the relations of the central government to the states? (Elliot, ed., *The Debates in the Several State Conventions, on the Adoption of the Constitution*, I, 327–31.) The numbers have been added.]

[Preamble]
Amendments Proposed by New York Convention
July 26, 1788

WE THE Delegates of the People of the State of New York . . . Do declare and make known.

[1]   That all Power is originally vested in and consequently derived from the People, and that Government is instituted by them for their common Interest Protection and Security.

[2]   That the enjoyment of Life, Liberty and the pursuit of Happiness are essential rights which every Government ought to respect and preserve.

[3]   That the Powers of Government may be reassumed by the People, whensoever it shall become necessary to their Happiness; that every Power, Jurisdiction and right, which is not by the said Constitution clearly delegated to the Congress of the United States, or the departments of the Government thereof, remains to the People of the several States, or to their respective State Governments to whom they may have granted the same; And that those Clauses in the said Constitution, which declare, that Congress shall not have or exercise certain Powers, do not imply that Congress is entitled to any Powers not given by the said Constitution; but such Clauses are to be construed either as exceptions to certain specified Powers, or as inserted merely for greater Caution.

[4]   That the People have an equal, natural and unalienable right, freely and peaceably to Exercise their Religion according to the dictates of Conscience, and that no Religious Sect or Society ought to be favoured or established by Law in preference of others.

[5]   That the People have a right to keep and bear Arms; that a well regulated Militia, including the body of the People *capable of bearing Arms,* is the proper, natural and safe defence of a free State;

[6]   That the Militia should not be subject to Martial Law except in time of War, Rebellion or Insurrection.

[7]   That standing Armies in time of Peace are dangerous to Liberty, and ought not to be kept up, except in Cases of necessity; and that

at all times, the Military should be under strict Subordination to the civil Power.

[8] That in time of Peace no Soldier ought to be quartered in any House without the consent of the Owner, and in time of War only by the Civil Magistrate in such manner as the Laws may direct.

[9] That no Person ought to be taken imprisoned or disseised of his freehold, or be exiled or deprived of his Privileges, Franchises, Life, Liberty or Property but by due process of Law.

[10] That no Person ought to be put twice in Jeopardy of Life or Limb for one and the same Offence, nor, unless in case of impeachment, be punished more than once for the same Offence.

[11] That every Person restrained of his Liberty is entitled to an enquiry into the lawfulness of such restraint, and to a removal thereof if unlawful, and that such enquiry and removal ought not to be denied or delayed, except when on account of Public Danger the Congress shall suspend the privilege of the Writ of *Habeas Corpus*.

[12] That excessive Bail ought not to be required; nor excessive Fines imposed; nor Cruel or unusual Punishments inflicted.

[13] That (except in the Government of the Land and Naval Forces, and of the Militia when in actual Service, and in cases of Impeachment) a Presentment or Indictment by a Grand Jury ought to be observed as a necessary preliminary to the trial of all Crimes cognizable by the Judiciary of the United States, and such Trial should be speedy, public, and by an impartial Jury of the County where the Crime was committed; and that no person can be found Guilty without the unanimous consent of such Jury. But in cases of Crimes not committed within any County of any of the United States, and in Cases of Crimes committed within any County in which a general Insurrection may prevail, or which may be in the possession of a foreign Enemy, the enquiry and trial may be in such County as the Congress shall by Law direct; which County in the two Cases last mentioned should be as near as conveniently may be to that County in which the Crime may have been committed. And that in All Criminal Prosecutions, the Accused ought to be informed of the cause and nature of his Accusation, to be confronted with his accusers and the Witnesses against him, to have the means of producing his Witnesses, and the assistance of counsel for his defence, and should not be compelled to give Evidence against himself.

[14] That the trial by Jury in the extent that it obtains by the Common Law of England is one of the greatest securities to the rights of a free People, and ought to remain inviolate.

[15] That every Freeman has a right to be secure from all unreasonable searches and seizures of his person his papers or his property, and therefore, that all Warrants to search suspected places or seize any Freeman his papers or property, without information upon Oath or Affirmation of sufficient cause, are grievous and oppressive; and that all general Warrants (or such in which the place or person suspected are not particularly designated) are dangerous and ought not to be granted.

[16] That the People have a right peaceably to assemble together to consult for their common good, or to instruct their Representatives;

and that every person has a right to Petition or apply to the Legislature for redress of Grievances.—That the Freedom of the Press ought not to be violated or restrained.

[17]   That there should be once in four years an Election of the President and Vice President, so that no Officer who may be appointed by the Congress to act as President in case of the removal, death, resignation or inability of the President and Vice President can in any case continue to act beyond the termination of the period for which the last President and Vice President were elected.

[18]   That nothing contained in the said Constitution is to be construed to prevent the Legislature of any State from passing Laws at its discretion from time to time to divide such State into convenient Districts, and to apportion its Representatives to and amongst such Districts.

[19]   That the Prohibition contained in the said Constitution against *ex post facto* Laws, extends only to Laws concerning Crimes.

[20]   That all Appeals in Causes determinable according to the course of the common Law, ought to be by Writ of Error and not otherwise.

[21]   That the Judicial Power of the United States in cases in which a State may be a party, does not extend to criminal Prosecutions, or to authorize any Suit by any Person against a State.

[22]   That the Judicial Power of the United States as to Controversies between Citizens of the same State claiming Lands under Grants of different States is not to be construed to extend to any other controversies between them except those which relate to such Lands, so claimed under Grants of different States.

[23]   That the Jurisdiction of the Supreme Court of the United States, or of any other Court to be instituted by the Congress, is not in any case to be increased enlarged or extended by any Fiction Collusion or mere suggestion;—And That no Treaty is to be construed so to operate as to alter the Constitution of any State. . . .

[Changes in the Body of the Constitution]

And the Convention do in the Name and Behalf of the People of the State of New York enjoin it upon their Representatives in the Congress, to Exert all their Influence, and use all reasonable means to Obtain a Ratification of the following Amendments to the said Constitution in the manner prescribed therein; and in all Laws to be passed by the Congress in the meantime to conform to the spirit of the said Amendments as far as the Constitution will admit.

[1]   That there shall be one Representative for every thirty thousand Inhabitants, according to the enumeration or Census mentioned in the Constitution, until the whole number of Representatives amounts to two hundred; after which that number shall be continued or increased but not diminished, as Congress shall direct, and according to such ratio as the Congress shall fix, in conformity to the rule prescribed for the Apportionment of Representatives and direct Taxes.

[2] That the Congress do not impose any Excise on any Article (except Ardent Spirits) of the Growth Production or Manufacture of the United States, or any of them.

[3] That Congress do not lay direct Taxes but when the Monies arising from the Impost and Excise shall be insufficient for the Public Exigencies, nor then until Congress shall first have made a Requisition upon the States to assess levy and pay their respective proportions of such Requisition, agreeable to the Census fixed in the said Constitution, in such way and manner as the Legislatures of the respective States shall judge best; and in such Case, if any State shall neglect or refuse to pay its proportion pursuant to such Requisition, then Congress may assess and levy such state's proportion, together with Interest at the rate of six per Centum per Annum, from the time of Payment prescribed in such Requisition.

[4] That the Congress shall not make or alter any Regulation in any State respecting the times places and manner of holding Elections for Senators or Representatives, unless the Legislature of such State shall neglect or refuse to make Laws or Regulations for the purpose, or from any circumstance be incapable of making the same; and then only until the Legislature of such State shall make provision in the premises; provided that Congress may prescribe the time for the Election of Representatives.

[5] That no Persons except natural born Citizens, or such as were Citizens on or before the fourth day of July one thousand seven hundred and seventy six, or such as held Commissions under the United States during the War, and have at any time since the fourth day of July one thousand seven hundred and seventy six become Citizens of one or other of the United States, and who shall be Freeholders, shall be eligible to the Places of President, Vice President, or Members of either House of the Congress of the United States.

[6] That the Congress do not grant Monopolies or erect any Company with exclusive Advantages of Commerce.

[7] That no standing Army or regular Troops shall be raised or kept up in time of peace, without the consent of two-thirds of the Senators and Representatives present, in each House.

[8] That no Money be borrowed on the Credit of the United States without the Assent of two-thirds of the Senators and Representatives present in each House.

[9] That the Congress shall not declare War without the concurrence of two-thirds of the Senators and Representatives present in each House.

[10] That the Privilege of the *Habeas Corpus* shall not by any Law be suspended for a longer term than six Months, or until twenty days after the Meeting of the Congress next following the passing of the Act for such suspension.

[11] That the Right of the Congress to exercise exclusive Legislation over such District, not exceeding ten Miles square, as may by cession of a particular State, and the acceptance of Congress, become the Seat of the Government of the United States, shall not be so exer-

cised, as to exempt the Inhabitants of such District from paying the like Taxes Imposts Duties and Excises, as shall be imposed on the other Inhabitants of the State in which such District may be; and that no person shall be privileged within the said District from Arrest for Crimes committed, or Debts contracted out of the said District.

[12]   That the Right of exclusive Legislation with respect to such places as may be purchased for the Erection of Forts, Magazines, Arsenals, Dockyards and other needful Buildings, shall not authorize the Congress to make any Law to prevent the Laws of the States respectively in which they may be, from extending to such places in all civil and Criminal Matters except as to such Persons as shall be in the Service of the United States; nor to them with respect to Crimes committed without such Places.

[13]   That the Compensation for the Senators and Representatives be ascertained by standing Laws; and that no alteration of the existing rate of Compensation shall operate for the Benefit of the Representatives, until after a subsequent Election shall have been had.

[14]   That the Journals of the Congress shall be published at least once a year, with the exception of such parts relating to Treaties or Military operations, as in the Judgment of either House shall require Secrecy; and that both Houses of Congress shall always keep their Doors open during their Sessions, unless the Business may in their Opinion require Secrecy. That the yeas & nays shall be entered on the Journals whenever two Members in either House may require it.

[15]   That no Capitation Tax shall ever be laid by the Congress.

[16]   That no Person be eligible as a Senator for more than six years in any term of twelve years; and that the Legislatures of the respective States may recall their Senators or either of them, and elect others in their stead, to serve the remainder of the time for which the Senators so recalled were appointed.

[17]   That no Senator or Representative shall during the time for which he was elected be appointed to any Office under the Authority of the United States.

[18]   That the Authority given to the Executives of the States to fill the vacancies of Senators be abolished, and that such vacancies be filled by the respective Legislatures.

[19]   That the Power of Congress to pass uniform Laws concerning Bankruptcy shall only extend to Merchants and other Traders; and that the States respectively may pass Laws for the relief of other Insolvent Debtors.

[20]   That no Person shall be eligible to the Office of President of the United States a third time.

[21]   That the Executive shall not grant Pardons for Treason, unless with the Consent of the Congress; but may at his discretion grant Reprieves to persons convicted of Treason, until their Cases, can be laid before the Congress.

[22]   That the President or person exercising his Powers for the time being, shall not command an Army in the Field in person, without the previous desire of the Congress.

[23] That all Letters Patent, Commissions, Pardons, Writs and Process of the United States, shall run in the Name of *the People of the United States,* and be tested in the Name of the President of the United States, or the person exercising his powers for the time being, or the first Judge of the Court out of which the same shall issue, as the case may be.

[24] That the Congress shall not constitute ordain or establish any Tribunals or Inferior Courts, with any other than Appellate Jurisdiction, except such as may be necessary for the trial of Causes of Admiralty and Maritime Jurisdiction, and for the Trial of Piracies and Felonies committed on the High Seas; and in all other Cases to which the Judicial Power of the United States extends, and in which the Supreme Court of the United States has not original Jurisdiction, the Causes shall be heard tried, and determined in some one of the State Courts, with the right of Appeal to the Supreme Court of the United States, or other proper Tribunal to be established for that purpose by the Congress, with such exceptions, and under such regulations as the Congress shall make.

[26] That persons aggrieved by any Judgment, Sentence or Decree of the Supreme Court of the United States, in any Cause in which that Court has original Jurisdiction, with such exceptions and under such Regulations as the Congress shall make concerning the same, shall upon application, have a Commission to be issued by the President of the United States, to such Men learned in the Law as he shall nominate, and by and with the Advice and consent of the Senate appoint, not less than seven, authorizing such Commissioners, or any seven or more of them, to correct the Errors in such Judgment or to review such Sentence and Decree, as the case may be, and to do Justice to the parties in the Premises.

[27] That no Judge of the Supreme Court of the United States shall hold any other Office under the United States, or any of them.

[28] That the Judicial Power of the United States shall extend to no Controversies respecting Land, unless it relate to Claims of Territory or Jurisdiction between States, or to Claims of Land between Individuals, or between States and Individuals under the Grants of different States.

[29] That the Militia of any State shall not be compelled to serve without the limits of the State for a longer term than six weeks, without the Consent of the Legislature thereof.

[30] That the words *without the Consent of the Congress* in the seventh Clause of the ninth Section of the first Article of the Constitution, be expunged.

[31] That the Senators and Representatives and all Executive and Judicial Officers of the United States shall be bound by Oath or Affirmation not to infringe or violate the Constitutions or Rights of the respective States.

[32] That the Legislatures of the respective States may make Provision by Law, that the Electors of the Election Districts to be by them appointed shall choose a Citizen of the United States who shall

have been an Inhabitant of such District for the Term of one year immediately preceding the time of his Election, for one of the Representatives of such State.

C.

ABRAHAM YATES OBJECTS TO THE RESULTS

❡To weigh the two sides of the anti-Federalist controversy, one must take note of the results of the struggle for amendments, which were clear by 1790. The point of view of the "non-adopting" anti-Federalists in New York can be traced in these excerpts from articles of Abraham Yates, an influential upstate leader who wrote under the pseudonymn of "Rough Hewer." Without naming him, Yates is criticizing Smith and raising the question of whether his tactics were correct, the same question the reader can ponder.

1. *December, 1788.* (An open letter, "To the Members of the Legislature of the State of New York," December 8, 1788, Yates Papers, New York Public Library.)]

IT IS said on the one hand that they [the anti-Federalist members of the ratifying convention] were seduced and deceived by fears of convulsions, anarchy and confusion, and that Congress would remove out of the State if it should not be adopted and on the other that they adopted it from an invincible reluctance to a separation from our sister states. It is sufficient to know that it has been adopted in the full confidence that amendments would take place and that there were gentlemen for and against the measure. Which were right and which wrong time and experience would determine. . . .

[2. *Spring, 1789.* A second convention was not called; the Federalists instead decided they would take up amendments in the new Congress, which they controlled, and then submit them to the states. When Federalists disparaged the need for amendments, Yates wrote an angry history of the movement for the Constitution indicting it as a "conspiracy." ("Abraham Yates's History of the Movement for the United States Constitution," Staughton Lynd, ed., *William and Mary Quarterly*, 3rd. series, XX [April, 1963], 242–45. Reprinted with the permission of the Institute of Early American History and Culture.)]

THE MEETING at Philadelphia in 1787 for the sole and express purpose of revising the Articles of Confederation, got the name of a Convention (I believe before long that of a Conspiracy would have been more Significant), [and] paid no more regard to their orders and credentials than Caesar when he passed the Rubicon. Under an Injunction of Secrecy they carried on their works of Darkness untill the Constitution passed their usurping hands.

It did not pass through Congress without an attempt for an approbation. When it was sent on to the respective states, [what] Management and Deceptions were used by the advocates in representing in their publications the perfection of the instrument, [what] meetings and processions of the different classes of the inhabitants (as if they wandered after and worshipped the Beast) to dupe, Infatuate and ensnare the unwary! [What] violence and Intrigue [was] used in other states: The members of the Legislature of Pennsylvania were dragged by violence, those of Rhode Island by menaces of the Higher powers, into the Measures; those of New Hampshire, Massachusetts, New York, Virginia and North Carolina were flattered and deceived; those of Massachusetts were made to believe that by making it a standing Instruction to their Members in Congress they would infallibly succeed! The Convention of New York went a step further in agreeing to write a Letter which was signed by every member of the Convention, Directed to every Legislature in the federal Union, expressive of the Indispensable Necessity of Speedy Amendments. All the Members in the Convention unanimously agreed to and Signed this Letter: those that have Religiously Done their Endeavors to perform their promises have acted Honorably.

I must confess I never heard that the Members of either Massachusetts or New York were more strenuous for amendments than those of other States; and if we judge from the prints, it appears that the one they try to frighten from the attempt, the other [they try to frighten] into despair. To this they insinuate that it is Dangerous to examin Systems of Government; to the others: You stand in a precarious situation, like that of the Priest in his flock (the Priest having by his call undertaken to supply them with Rain when they called for it, and when they did he said they must be unanimous). And we are told that there [are] not a few in every state who in their tender mercies, Rather than to amend the faults in the Constitution, would overset the whole and have another chance for an aristocracy. . . .

Upon the whole, if upon comparing the usurpation of the Crown of Great Britain upon the parliamentary Rights, with the usurpations of the American Congress upon the sovereignty of the individual states (which was the design of this discussion), upon the contrast I have made it appear (which I trust I have) that American Rulers, if not worse than British, are every way as likely to abuse their powers, to act the wolf in sheeps cloathing; [then] I submit whether it is not High time that we should be upon our guard, while we leave not a stone unturned to obtain the Necessary amendments to the new System, to avert the curse (Next to that of Adam) which we will Entail upon our Descendants without Amendments.

[3. *March, 1790.* After Congress submitted twelve amendments to the states, Yates compared them to those proposed by the New York convention and wrote the following article. ("Rough Hewer Notebook," March 15, 22, 1790, Yates Papers, New York Public Library.) Of these twelve the first two were not ratified, the remaining ten became the Bill of Rights. How many of their proposed amendments did the anti-Federalists get? In view of the outcome, what judgment should be made of Melancton Smith's tactics?]

THE AMENDMENTS agreed to in Congress and now offered to the State Legislature are the twelve following, which are or at least ought to be, in the hands of every well wisher to freedom.

Article the first . . . After the first enumeration required by the first Article of the Constitution, there shall be one Representative for every thirty thousand, until the number shall amount to one hundred, after which, the proportion shall be so regulated by Congress, that there shall be not less than one hundred Representatives nor less than one Representative for every forty thousand persons, until the number of Representatives shall amount to two hundred, after which the proportion shall be so regulated by Congress, that there shall not be less than two hundred Representatives, nor more than one Representative for every fifty thousand persons.

Article the second . . . No law, varying the compensation for the services of the Senators and Representatives, shall take effect, until an election of Representatives shall have intervened.

Article the third . . . Congress shall make no law respecting an establishment of religion, or prohibiting the free exercise thereof; or abridging the freedom of speech, or of the press, or the right of the people peaceably to assemble, and to petition the Government for a redress of grievances.

Article the fourth . . . A well regulated Militia, being necessary to the security of a free State, the right of the people to keep and bear Arms, shall not be infringed.

Article the fifth . . . No Soldier shall, in time of peace be quartered in any house, without the consent of the Owner, nor in time of war, but in a manner to be prescribed by law.

Article the sixth . . . The right of the people to be secure in their persons, houses, papers, and effects, against unreasonable searches and seizures, shall not be violated, and no Warrants shall issue, but upon probable cause, supported by Oath or affirmation, and particularly describing the place to be searched, and the persons or things to be seized.

Article the seventh . . . No person shall be held to answer for a capital, or otherwise infamous crime, unless on a presentment or indictment of a Grand Jury, except in cases arising in the land or naval forces, or in the Militia, when in actual service in time of War or public danger; nor shall any person be subject for the same offence to be twice put in jeopardy of life or limb, nor shall be compelled in any criminal case to be a witness against himself, nor be deprived of life, liberty, or property, without due process of law; nor shall private property be taken for public use without just compensation.

Article the eighth . . . In all criminal prosecutions, the accused shall enjoy the right to a speedy and public trial, by an impartial jury of the State and district wherein the crime shall have been committed, which district shall have been previously ascertained by law, and to be informed of the nature and cause of the accusation; to be confronted with the witnesses against him; to have compulsory process for obtaining witnesses in his favor, and to have the Assistance of Counsel for his defence.

Article the ninth . . . In suits at common law, where the value in controversy shall exceed twenty dollars, the right of trial by jury shall be preserved, and no fact tried by a jury shall be otherwise re-examined in any Court of the United States, than according to the rules of the common law.

Article the tenth . . . Excessive bail shall not be required, nor excessive fines imposed, nor cruel and unusual punishments inflicted.

Article the eleventh . . . The enumeration in the Constitution, of certain rights, shall not be construed to deny or disparage others retained by the people.

Article the twelfth . . . The powers not delegated to the United States by the Constitution, nor prohibited by it to the States, are reserved to the States respectively, or to the people.

These compared to the amendments of the State of New York . . . are unimportant or trivial at least to the people of this State. . . .

The Amendments proposed by the convention of New York are intended either to explain or restrict certain dangerous powers expressly or impliedly lodged in Congress . . . and why they do not appear among the amendments proposed may be the subject of further consideration.

NEITHER FEDERALIST NOR
ANTI-FEDERALIST

While the Constitution was under discussion Thomas Jefferson and Thomas Paine were in France—Jefferson as the American Minister, Paine to promote an iron bridge he had developed. Madison kept Jefferson informed; Paine visited with Jefferson, and, when the new Constitution arrived early in 1788, their friend, the Marquis de Lafayette, reported that the three of them debated the new plan of government "in a convention of our own as earnestly as if we were to decide upon it." (Lafayette to Henry Knox, February 4, 1788, quoted in Louis Gottschalk, *Lafayette Between the American and the French Revolution, 1783–1789* [Chicago: Univ. of Chicago Press, 1950] p. 374.)

Their views are in contrast to those already presented; indeed it is something of a problem as to what one should call them. In 1789 Jefferson protested to a friend, "I am not of the party of federalists. But I am much farther from that of the anti-federalists. . . . I am of neither party, nor yet a trimmer between parties." Their views are of special interest because they, as much as Patrick Henry or Melancton Smith, could claim to speak for the "middling classes" or "the yeomanry" against the "rich and well born." Indeed, both Paine and Jefferson are often regarded as outstanding spokesmen for the "democratic" point of view in the Revolution. What, then, was their opinion of the Constitution?

A.

THOMAS JEFFERSON ASKS FOR A BILL OF RIGHTS

❧Although Jefferson was a well-to-do planter, he had clearly identified himself with the goal of reform in his native Virginia. He had advocated a state constitution that would have given backcountry farmers more equal representation, a public educational system, and the gradual abolition of slavery—all without success. He had succeeded in eliminating the feudal relics of entail and primogeniture (although this did not "put an axe" to the landed aristocracy as he thought), in revising the code of laws, and in beginning the separation of church and state. His book, *Notes on Virginia*, made it clear that his ideal society was one of independent land-holding farmers who were educated and free to think and worship as they pleased, with as little government as possible. He was very much a Virginia man (Governor of the state, 1779–1781) and looked on the decentralized Articles of Confederation constitution as "a venerable old fabric."

After the war his experiences as Minister to France convinced him that more national strength was needed to protect American interests abroad. When he first heard of the meeting of the Philadelphia convention he wrote that "My general plan would be to make the states one as to every thing connected with foreign nations, and several as to everything purely domestic." When he received the new Constitution he confessed, "I find myself nearly a neutral. There is a great mass of good in it, in a very desirable form, but there is also to me a bitter pill, or two." (Jefferson to Carrington, August 4, 1787, December 21, 1787, in Boyd, ed., *The Papers of Thomas Jefferson*, XI, 678; XII, 446.) It was in this mood that he discussed the Constitution with Paine and began a lengthy exchange with Madison.

1. *Jefferson to Madison: "What I like"; "What I do not like."* (a letter, December 20, 1787, in Boyd, ed., *The Papers of Thomas Jefferson*, XII, 439–42.) What did he like in the new Constitution? What did he dislike, aside from the absence of a Bill of Rights? What general attitude to government did he reveal in this letter? Was Jefferson closer to the Federalists or to the anti-Federalists?]

THE SEASON admitting only of operations in the Cabinet, and these being in a great measure secret, I have little to fill a letter. I will therefore make up the deficiency by adding a few words on the Constitution proposed by our Convention. I like much the general idea of framing a government which should go on of itself peaceably, without needing continual recurrence to the state legislatures. I like the organization of the government into Legislative, Judiciary and Executive. I like the power given the Legislature to levy taxes; and for that reason solely approve of the greater house being chosen by the people directly. For tho' I think a house chosen by them will be very illy qualified to legislate for the Union, for foreign nations &c. yet this evil does not weigh against the good of preserving inviolate the fundamental principle that the people are not to be taxed but by representatives chosen immediately by themselves. I am captivated by the compromise of the opposite claims of the great and little states, of the latter to equal, and the former to proportional influence. I am much pleased too with the substitution of the method of voting by persons, instead of that of voting by states: and I like the negative given to the Executive with a third of either house, though I should have liked it better had the Judiciary been associated for that purpose, or invested with a similar and separate power. There are other good things of less moment.

I will now add what I do not like. First the omission of a bill of rights providing clearly and without the aid of sophisms for freedom of religion, freedom of the press, protection against standing armies, restriction against monopolies, the eternal and unremitting force of the habeas corpus laws, and trials by jury in all matters of fact triable by the laws of the land and not by the law of Nations. To say, as Mr. James Wilson does that a bill of rights was not necessary because all is reserved in the case of the general government which is not given, while in the particular ones all is given which is not reserved might do for the Audience to whom it was addressed, but is surely gratis dictum, opposed by strong inferences from the body of the instrument, as well as from the omission of the clause of our present confederation which had declared that in express terms. It was a hard conclusion to say because there has been no uniformity among the states as to the cases triable by the jury, because some have been so incautious as to abandon this mode of trial, therefore the more prudent states shall be reduced to the same level of calamity. It would have been much more just and wise to have concluded the other way that as most of the states had judiciously preserved this palladium, those who had wandered should be brought back to it, and to have established general right instead of general wrong. Let me add that a bill of rights is what the people are entitled to against every government on earth, general or particular, and what no just government should refuse, or rest on inference.

The second feature I dislike, and greatly dislike, is the abandonment in every instance of the necessity of rotation in office, and most particularly in the case of the President. Experience concurs with reason in concluding that the first magistrate will always be re-elected if the constitution permits it. He is then an officer for life. This once observed it becomes of so much consequence to certain nations to have a friend or a foe at the head of our affairs that they will interfere with money and with arms. A Galloman or an Angloman will be supported by the nation he befriends. If once elected, and at a second or third election outvoted by one or two votes, he will pretend false votes, foul play, hold possession of the reins of government, be supported by the states voting for him, especially if they are the central ones lying in a compact body themselves and separating their opponents: and they will be aided by one nation of Europe, while the majority are aided by another. The election of a President of America some years hence will be much more interesting to certain nations of Europe than ever the election of a king of Poland was. Reflect on all the instances in history ancient and modern, of elective monarchies, and say if they do not give foundation for my fears, the Roman emperors, the popes, while they were of any importance, the German emperors till they became hereditary in practice, the kings of Poland, the Deys of the Ottoman dependancies. It may be said that if elections are to be attended with these disorders, the seldomer they are renewed the better. But experience shews that the only way to prevent disorder is to render them uninteresting by frequent changes. An incapacity to be elected a second time would have been the only effectual preventative. The power of removing him every fourth year by the vote of the people is a power which will not be exercised. The king of Poland is removeable every day by the Diet, yet he is never removed.

Smaller objections are the Appeal in fact as well as law, and the binding all persons Legislative, Executive and Judiciary by oath to maintain that constitution. I do not pretend to decide what would be the best method of procuring the establishment of the manifold good things in this constitution, and of getting rid of the bad. Whether by adopting it in hopes of future amendment, or, after it has been duly weighed and canvassed by the people, after seeing the parts they generally dislike, and those they generally approve, to say to them, 'We see now what you wish. Send together your deputies again, let them frame a constitution for you omitting what you have condemned, and establishing the powers you approve. Even these will be a great addition to the energy of your government.'—At all events I hope you will not be discouraged from other trials, if the present one should fail of it's [sic] full effect.

I have thus told you freely what I like and dislike: merely as a matter of curiosity for I know your own judgment has been formed on all these points after having heard every thing which could be urged on them. I own I am not a friend to a very energetic government. It is always oppressive. The late rebellion in Massachusetts [Shays's Rebellion] has given more alarm than I think it should have done. Calculate that one rebellion in 13 states in the course of 11 years, is but one for each state in a century and a half. No country should be so long without one. Nor will any degree of power in the hands of government prevent insurrections. France with all it's [sic] despotism, and two or three hundred thousand men always in arms has had three insurrections in the three years I have been here in every one of which greater numbers were engaged than in Massachusetts and a great deal more blood was spilt. In Turkey, which Montesquieu supposes more despotic, insurrections are the events of every day. In England, where the hand of power is lighter than here, but heavier than with us they happen every half dozen years. Compare again the ferocious depredations of their insurgents with the order, the moderation and the almost self extinguishment of ours.

After all, it is my principle that the will of the Majority should always prevail. If they approve the proposed Convention in all it's [sic] parts, I shall concur in it chearfully [sic], in hopes that they will amend it whenever they shall find it work[s] wrong. I think our governments will remain virtuous for many centuries; as long as they are chiefly agricultural; and this will be as long as there shall be vacant lands in any part of America. When they get piled upon one another in large cities, as in Europe, they will become corrupt as in Europe. Above all things I hope the education of the common people will be attended to; convinced that on their good sense we may rely with the most security for the preservation of a due degree of liberty. I have tired you by this time with my disquisitions and will therefore only add assurances of the sincerity of those sentiments of esteem and attachment with which I am Dear Sir your affectionate friend & servant.

[2. *Madison to Jefferson: "The Inefficacy of Parchment Barriers."*
After ratification Madison sent Jefferson a pamphlet reprinting the proposed amendments and stated his views on a Bill of Rights. (A letter,
October 17, 1788, in Boyd, ed., *The Papers of Thomas Jefferson*, XIV,
18–21.) What was Madison's argument against a Bill of Rights? How far
apart was he from Jefferson?]

My own opinion has always been in favor of a bill of rights; provided it be so framed as not to imply powers not meant to be included
in the enumeration. At the same time I have never thought the omission
a material defect, nor been anxious to supply it even by subsequent
amendment, for any other reason than that it is anxiously desired by
others. I have favored it because I supposed it might be of use, and if
properly executed could not be of disservice. I have not viewed it in an
important light. 1. Because I conceive that in a certain degree, though
not in the extent argued by Mr. Wilson, the rights in question are
reserved by the manner in which the federal powers are granted. 2. Because there is great reason to fear that a positive declaration of some of
the most essential rights could not be obtained in the requisite latitude.
I am sure that the rights of conscience in particular, if submitted to
public definition would be narrowed much more than they are likely
ever to be by an assumed power. One of the objections in New England
was that the Constitution by prohibiting religious tests opened a door
for Jews Turks and infidels. 3. Because the limited powers of the federal
Government and the jealousy of the subordinate Governments, afford a
security which has not existed in the case of the State Governments,
and exists in no other. 4. Because experience proves the inefficacy of a
bill of rights on those occasions when its controul is most needed. Repeated violations of these parchment barriers have been committed by
overbearing majorities in every State. In Virginia I have seen the bill of
rights violated in every instance where it has been opposed to a popular
current. Notwithstanding the explicit provision contained in that instrument for the rights of Conscience it is well known that a religious
establishment would have taken place in that State, if the legislative
majority had found as they expected, a majority· of the people in favor
of the measure; and I am persuaded that if a majority of the people were
now of one sect, the measure would still take place and on narrower
ground than was then proposed, notwithstanding the additional obstacle
which the law has since created. . . .

[3. *Jefferson to Madison: "A Brace to Keep up the Building."* Jefferson took up Madison's arguments point by point. (A letter, March 15,
1789, in Boyd, ed., *The Papers of Thomas Jefferson*, XIV, 659–61.)
What were Jefferson's specific answers to Madison? Who had the better
argument? Does Jefferson's attitude toward the Constitution at the end
of this letter show any change?]

Your thoughts on the subject of the Declaration of rights in the
letter of Oct. 17. I have weighed with great satisfaction. Some of them

had not occurred to me before, but were acknoleged [*sic*] just in the moment they were presented to my mind. In the arguments in favor of a declaration of rights, you omit one which has great weight with me, the legal check which it puts into the hands of the judiciary. This is a body, which if rendered independent, and kept strictly to their own department merits great confidence for their learning and integrity. In fact what degree of confidence would be too much for a body composed of such men as Wythe, Blair, and Pendleton? On characters like these the 'civium ardor prava jubentium' would make no impression. I am happy to find that on the whole you are a friend to this amendment. The Declaration of rights is like all other human blessings alloyed with some inconveniences, and not accomplishing fully it's [*sic*] object. But the good in this instance vastly overweighs the evil. I cannot refrain from making short answers to the objections which your letter states to have been raised.

1. That the rights in question are reserved by the manner in which the federal powers are granted. Answer. A constitutive act may certainly be so formed as to need no declaration of rights. The act itself has the force of a declaration as far as it goes: and if it goes to all material points nothing more is wanting. In the draught of a constitution which I had once a thought of proposing in Virginia, and printed afterwards, I endeavored to reach all the great objects of public liberty, and did not mean to add a declaration of rights. Probably the object was imperfectly executed: but the deficiencies would have been supplied by others in the course of discussion. But in a constitutive act which leaves some precious articles unnoticed, and raises implications against others, a declaration of rights becomes necessary by way of supplement. This is the case of our new federal constitution. This instrument forms us into one state as to certain objects, and gives us a legislative and executive body for these objects. It should therefore guard us against their abuses of power within the field submitted to them.

2. A positive declaration of some essential rights could not be obtained in the requisite latitude. Answer. Half a loaf is better than no bread. If we cannot secure all our rights, let us secure what we can.

3. The limited powers of the federal government and jealousy of the subordinate governments afford a security which exists in no other instance. Answer. The first member of this seems resolvable into the 1st. objection before stated. The jealousy of the subordinate governments is a precious reliance. But observe that those governments are only agents. They must have principles furnished them whereon to found their opposition. The declaration of rights will be the text whereby they will try all the acts of the federal government. In this view it is necessary to the federal government also: as by the same text they may try the opposition of the subordinate governments.

4. Experience proves the inefficacy of a bill of rights. True. But tho it is not absolutely efficacious under all circumstances, it is of great potency always, and rarely inefficacious. A brace the more will often keep up the building which would have fallen with that brace the less.

There is a remarkeable difference between the characters of the Inconveniencies which attend a Declaration of rights, and those which attend the want of it. The inconveniencies of the Declaration are that it may cramp government in it's [*sic*] useful exertions. But the evil of this is shortlived, moderate, and reparable. The inconveniencies of the want of a Declaration are permanent, afflicting and irreparable: they are in constant progression from bad to worse. The executive in our governments is not the sole, it is scarcely the principal object of my jealousy. The tyranny of the legislatures is the most formidable dread at present, and will be for long years. That of the executive will come in it's [*sic*] turn, but it will be at a remote period. I know there are some among us who would now establish a monarchy. But they are inconsiderable in number and weight of character. The rising race are all republicans. We were educated in royalism: no wonder if some of us retain that idolatry still. Our young people are educated in republicanism. An apostacy from that to royalism is unprecedented and impossible. I am much pleased with the prospect that a declaration of rights will be added: and hope it will be done in that way which will not endanger the whole frame of the government, or any essential part of it.

B.

THOMAS PAINE ASKS FOR "A HOOP FOR THE BARREL"

❧If Jefferson represented the view of "agrarian democracy," Paine came closest among the Founding Fathers to being a spokesman for the "mechanic" classes of the cities—for the men who marched for the Constitution in the New York City parade described in Chapter I. He himself was of plebeian origins having held a variety of humble jobs in England before he came to the colonies in 1774. In 1776 he was rocketed to fame overnight for his pamphlet *Common Sense* which turned the tide of opinion toward independence and argued for a popularly elected national government. Throughout his life Paine wrote in a rough, vigorous style that appealed to the common man. Unlike Jefferson or Melancton Smith, during the Revolution he championed the cause of both democracy and strong central government. He defended the liberal constitution of Pennsylvania as "good for a poor man" and also complained that "the continental belt is too loosely buckled." In the 1790's he would rise to the heights of fame for his book *The Rights of Man*, defending the French Revolution, and for *The Age of Reason*, criticizing organized religion.

In their little "convention" in Paris, Paine shared Jefferson's concern for the Bill of Rights. He also had other criticisms of the new government. But unlike Jefferson, he seems to have been more emphatic that the constitution should be adopted with all of its faults. He set down his views a few years later in a newspaper article in which he objected strenuously to the attacks on himself as an "anti-Federalist." ("A Letter to George Washington," July 30, 1796, in Philip Foner, ed., *The Complete Writings of Thomas Paine* [New York: Citadel Press, 1945], II, 691–93. Reprinted with the permission of the publisher.) What were Paine's objections to the Constitution? Why was he for it?]

At the time I left America (April, 1787) the Continental Convention, that formed the Federal Constitution was on the point of meeting. Since that time new schemes of politics, and new distinctions of parties have arisen. The term *Anti-federalist* has been applied to all those who combated the defects of that Constitution, or opposed the measures of your administration.

It was only to the absolute necessity of establishing some Federal authority, extending equally over all States, that an instrument so inconsistent as the present Federal Constitution is, obtained a suffrage. I would have voted for it myself, had I been in America, or even for a worse, rather than have had none, provided it contained the means of remedying its defects by the same appeal to the people by which it was to be established. It is always better policy to leave removable errors to expose themselves than to hazard too much in contending against them theoretically.

I have introduced these observations, not only to mark the general difference between Anti-federalist and Anti-constitutionalist, but to preclude the effect, and even the application, of the former of these terms to myself.

I declare myself opposed to several matters in the Constitution, particularly to the manner in which what is called the Executive is formed, and to the long duration of the Senate; and if I live to return to America, I will use all my endeavors to have them altered. I also declare myself opposed to almost the whole of your administration; for I know it to have been deceitful, if not perfidious, as I shall show in the course of this letter.

But as to the point of consolidating the States into a Federal Government, it so happens, that the proposition for that purpose came originally from myself. I proposed it in a letter to Chancellor Livingston in the spring of 1782, while that gentleman was Minister for Foreign Affairs. The five per cent. duty recommended by Congress had then fallen through, having been adopted by some of the States, altered by others, rejected by Rhode Island, and repealed by Virginia after it had been consented to.

The proposal in the letter I allude to, was to get over the whole difficulty at once, by annexing a Continental legislative body to Congress; for in order to have any law of the Union uniform, the case could only be that either Congress, as it then stood, must frame the law, and the States severally adopt it without alteration, or the States must erect a Continental legislature for the purpose. . . .

After this account of a fact, the leaders of your party will scarcely have the hardiness to apply to me the term of Anti-federalist. But I can go to a date and to a fact beyond this; for the proposition for electing a Continental convention to form the Continental Government is one of the subjects treated of in the pamphlet "Common Sense."

Having thus cleared away a little of the rubbish that might otherwise have lain in my way, I return to the point of time at which the present Federal Constitution and your administration began.

It was very well said by an anonymous writer in Philadelphia, about a year before that period, that "thirteen staves and ne'er a hoop will not make a barrel," and as any kind of hooping the barrel, however defectively executed, would be better than none, it was scarcely possible but that considerable advantages must arise from the Federal hooping of the States. It was with pleasure that every sincere friend of America beheld, as the natural effect of union, her rising prosperity; and it was with grief they saw that prosperity mixed, even in the blossom, with the germ of corruption.

FOR FURTHER READING

For the student who wants to consult additional original source materials, they are plentiful for the three stages of the debate on the Constitution. For the debate at the Philadelphia Convention where the Constitution was drafted there is Max Farrand, ed., *The Records of the Federal Convention of 1787*, 4 vols. (rev. ed.; New Haven, Conn.: Yale Univ. Press, 1937), and a convenient compilation, Saul K. Padover, ed., *To Secure These Blessings: The Great Debates of the Constitutional Convention, Arranged According to Topics* (New York: Washington Square, 1962). For the public debate that followed, the indispensable *Federalist* essays by Hamilton, Jay, and Madison are in many inexpensive editions. Anti-Federalist pamphlets are in two books edited by Paul L. Ford, *Pamphlets on the Constitution of the United States* (Brooklyn, 1888), and *Essays on the Constitution of the United States* (Brooklyn, 1892). For the debates in the ratifying conventions see Jonathan Elliot, ed., *The Debates in the Several State Conventions, on the Adoption of the Constitution*, 5 vols. (1st ed., 1836).

To understand the historians' discussion of the subject one might begin with Charles Beard's famous work, *An Economic Interpretation of the Constitution of the United States* (New York: Macmillan, 1913; 2nd ed., 1935 and 1961). One can turn next to his critics, Robert E. Brown, *Charles Beard and the Constitution: A Critical Analysis of "An Economic Interpretation of the Constitution"* (Princeton, N.J.: Princeton Univ. Press, 1956), and especially Forrest McDonald, *We The People: The Economic Origins of the Constitution* (Chicago: Univ. of Chicago Press, 1958). Then one should turn to the critics of the critics: Lee Benson, *Turner and Beard: American Historical Writing Reconsidered* (Glencoe, Ill.: Fress Press, 1960), and Jackson T. Main, "A Critical Review of Forrest McDonald's *We The People*," *William and Mary Quarterly*, 3rd series, XVII (1960), 86–110, accompanied by a rebuttal by McDonald.

Jackson T. Main's book, *The Anti-Federalists: Critics of the Constitution, 1781–1788* (Chapel Hill: Univ. of North Carolina Press, 1961), may be contrasted with Cecelia Kenyon, "Men of Little Faith: The Anti-Federalists on the Nature of Representative Government," *William and Mary Quarterly*, 3rd series, XII (1955), 3–43. A short monograph, Staughton Lynd, *Anti-Federalism in Dutchess County, New York: A Study of Democracy and Class Conflict on the Revolutionary Era* (Chicago: Loyola Univ. Press, 1962), is valuable for its insight into Melanc-ton Smith, New York and the much abused subject of its subtitle.

The best biographies of the men whose opinions were presented are: Madison, Irving Brant; Henry, Robert D. Meade or Moses C. Tyler; Hamilton, Broadus Mitchell or John C. Miller; Jefferson, Dumas Malone or Adrienne Koch; Paine, Alfred Aldridge or Moncure Conway; for Smith, as for the others, see the valuable sketches in the *Dictionary of American Biography*. The original writings of these men are referred to in the notes above.

I wish to express my appreciation to Jackson T. Main, Staughton Lynd, and Robin Brooks as to suggestions for sources.

PRINTED IN U.S.A.

Date Due

MAR 28 '67			
DEC 14 '7			
NOV 1			
MAR 8 1984			
APR 5 1984			
NOV 9 1988			

Demco 293-5